The Lienzo of Tulancingo, Oaxaca

An Introductory Study of a Ninth Painted Sheet
From the Coixtlahuaca Valley

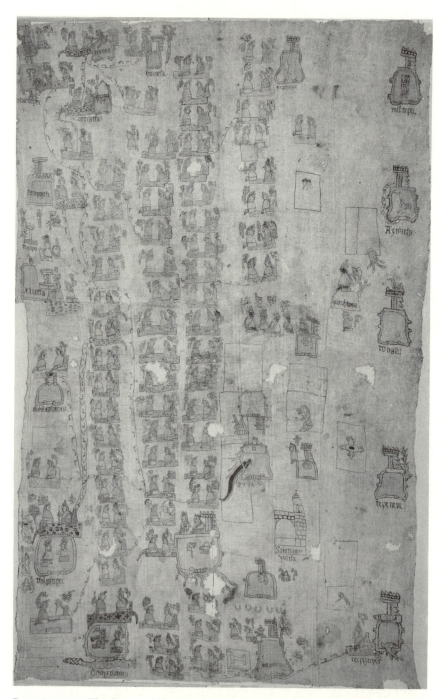

FRONTISPIECE. The lienzo of Ihuitlan Plumas, Oaxaca, Mexico. This great decorated sheet, nine feet high by five feet wide, was acquired by the Brooklyn Museum in 1941. The town lost it in 1900 and for many years it was owned by William Randolph Hearst. (Courtesy of the Brooklyn Museum, Carll H. de Silver Fund)

TRANSACTIONS

of the

American Philosophical Society

Held at Philadelphia for Promoting Useful Knowledge

VOLUME 83, Part 7, 1993

The Lienzo of Tulancingo, Oaxaca
An Introductory Study of a Ninth Painted Sheet From the Coixtlahuaca Valley

ROSS PARMENTER

THE AMERICAN PHILOSOPHICAL SOCIETY

Independence Square, Philadelphia

1993

Library of Congress Catalog
Card Number: 93-73287
International Standard Book Number 0-87169-837-4
US ISSN 0065-9746

TABLE OF CONTENTS

ILLUSTRATIONS

A MYSTERY SOLVED

History, especially ancient history, gains reality when it can be related to modern geography. The interplay will appear in instances cited throughout this study—specifically of Mexican geographical identifications that help recover segments of the country's pre-Columbian past. The study's principal aim, however, is not to discuss a broad theme, but to provide a new example. To be explicit, I hope to show how a particular identification augments the history that can be extracted from a related group of Mexican pictorial manuscripts, whose historical value, though well recognized, has as yet been little explored. I refer to the lienzos—genealogical, historical and geographical documents painted on cloth—of the Coixtlahuaca Valley in the northern region of the state of Oaxaca known as the Mixteca Alta (Fig. 1). The identification at issue is that of an important place called "Agua" by Alfonso Caso (1961, 246), the greatest of Mexican codex scholars, who did not know its real name. Running water in the town's emblem prompted his idea. The town is one of three in the Coixtlahuaca Valley represented with a major genealogy on the lienzo of Ihuitlan Plumas in the Brooklyn Museum, N.Y. (Frontispiece).

"Agua," it can now be reported, is the town of San Miguel Tulancingo which can be found in Figure 2, south of Ihuitlan and northwest of Coixtlahuaca, the other two towns on the lienzo with lengthy genealogies, or "ruler lists."

Lienzos are the names given the pictorial documents. The term comes from the Spanish word for any large sheet, either of cotton or linen, and often it is used for a European oil painting on canvas. But among scholars in Mexico it has acquired a particular meaning. By the time Spaniards arrived in Mexico in 1519, Mesoamericans had not yet invented an alphabet, but they had learned how to keep records in picture writing. They had also developed a form of feudalism, which in the case of the Aztecs, was developing into an ever expanding imperialism. Mexico was populous, and the Spanish conquerors were few. How were those Spaniards to rule and control so many new vassals? They did so by exploiting native rulers to keep their people peaceful and productive citizens of Spain by allowing them to rule relatively undisturbed in enjoyment of their lands, their serfs, their tributes and their privileges. Spain made it profitable for the regional lords to rule their own people; they bribed them, in other words, by buying them out by not deducting all the power and wealth acquired from their serfs. Because the Spaniards were determined to rule their new dominions by law, and in an orderly manner, this involved a lot of bookkeeping. And here the well-developed picture

1

FIGURE 1.   Map of the state of Oaxaca, showing the location of the Valley of Coixtlahuaca.

writing of the higher Mesoamerican cultures came in handy for both sides. Local lords could substantiate their claims to long possession of their lands and feudatories; doing so by mapping their ancestral territories and listing who their ancestors were. The Spaniards, in turn, could know who would rule what regions for them, and who would serve as their tribute collectors.

With so much information to be preserved, large cotton sheets proved more practical areas on which to paint the pictures of many rulers and places than the more constricted narrow strips of animal hide commonly used for records in pre-Conquest days. So the lienzo was invented, a type of document that, by being a combined map and pictorial history, proved especially useful in revealing geographical and historical relationships. The names of the rulers and the places they ruled have been the chief means of deciphering these sheets. Rulers and places were both depicted in the first post-Conquest decades in the manner worked out in pre-Conquest years. They had to be depicted thus at the start of the colonial period—pictorially, that is. The natives, lacking an alphabet of written symbols, could not set them down in any other manner; and the pictures, most of them realistic, became fairly easy for the Spaniards to interpret.

The depiction of places was managed by inventing symbols for those that have come to be known as place glyphs. The concept of the glyphs can be illustrated in modern times by, for example, the Statue of Liberty, the Eiffel Tower and Big Ben as symbols for New York, Paris and London.

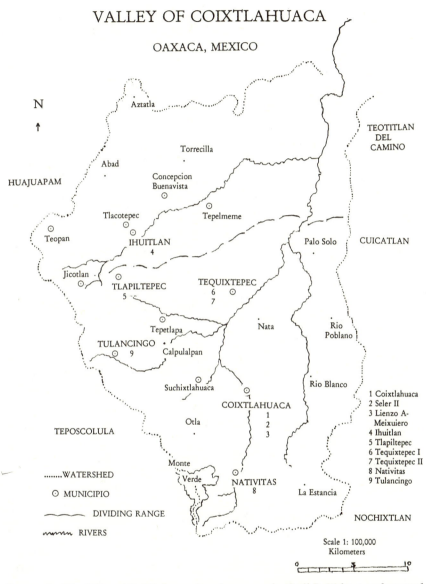

VALLEY OF COIXTLAHUACA

OAXACA, MEXICO

N
↑

TEOTITLAN
DEL
CAMINO

Aztatla

Torrecilla

Abad

Concepcion
Buenavista

HUAJUAPAM

Tlacotepec

Tepelmeme

Teopan

IHUITLAN
4

Palo Solo   CUICATLAN

Jicotlan

TLAPILTEPEC
5

TEQUIXTEPEC
6
7

Tepetlapa   Nata   Rio
Poblano

TULANCINGO
9   Calpulalpan

Suchixtlahuaca   Rio Blanco

COIXTLAHUACA
1
2
3

1 Coixtlahuaca
2 Seler II
3 Lienzo A-
   Meixuiero
4 Ihuitlan
5 Tlapiltepec
6 Tequixtepec I
7 Tequixtepec II
8 Nativitas
9 Tulancingo

TEPOSCOLULA

Otla

Monte
Verde

NATIVITAS
8

La Estancia

......WATERSHED

⊙ MUNICIPIO

———— DIVIDING RANGE

〰〰 RIVERS

NOCHIXTLAN

Scale 1: 100,000
Kilometers

0   5   10

FIGURE 2.   The Valley of Coixtlahuaca, based on a map by Cecil R. Welte, supplemented by a map of "Zona Coixtlahuaca Nochixtlan de la Mixteca Oaxaqueña" issued by the Papaloapam Commission of the Secretaria de Recursos Hidraulicos, provided by Ing. Jesús Franco Carrasco in 1974.

FIGURE 3.   The founders of San Miguel Tulancingo ("Agua"), Lord 6 Rain and Lady 10 Flint, as shown on the lienzo of Ihuitlan Plumas. Redrawn, as are other details from the lienzos, by the author.

And it can be assumed that the glyphs standing for important pre-Columbian towns also became well known to their contemporaries. All have pictorial elements. Because many towns were on hills, one finds many glyphs resembling sugar loafs, with outlines whose bases suggest scrolls in-curling at each side. Generally they are given individuality by adding a building, or a geographical feature, such as a river or a plant. Luckily, in some instances scribes, knowing or having learned European script, have identified the towns pictured by glossing them with their names. Glyphs have proved a principal tool of decipherment. Almost thirty can be located in the frontispiece. And one, the glyph for Tulancingo, with the shell-tipped streams, appears in detail in Figure 3.

The geography covered by our particular lienzos is shown from far away in Figure 1, where diagonal hatching locates the Valley of Coixtlahuaca. Its highest point is Monte Verde in the lower left (Figure 2) corner and the placement of the settlements is determined by its rivers. They, in turn, are fixed by the mildly rolling ridge that divides the valley into two basins. Because of this ridge, the streambed of the northern river, running north-east by Ihuitlan, is distinct from the larger river system. This more important system has a branch flowing by Tulancingo, and another by Coixtla-huaca. It is remarkable that so many pre-Columbian settlements have survived within a relatively small area after so many centuries. Actually, more exist than are on the map, but, to avoid confusion, the smallest have been omitted. Other archaeological remains and early records reveal that before the Spaniards came there were even more communities. The Spaniards "congregated" some into others, while some have disappeared. The six towns attended by numbers on Figure 3 are those whose overlords are known to have commissioned artists to create lienzos. To distinguish the documents of towns we will italicize them when referring to them.

On the lienzo *Ihuitlan* (Frontispiece) Coixtlahuaca is glossed as "cuyayxt-lavaca," and Ihuitlan (probably in an earlier location) as "pinoyalco yuitla," both glosses being visible at the lower edge of the frontispiece. Tulancingo, however, is not named, and that "Agua" should not be identified as Tulancingo is understandable. Not only does the glyph of Tulancingo have no gloss on *Ihuitlan*, but it bears no relation to the way Tulancingo's glyph is depicted on four other lienzos of the Coixtlahuaca Valley (Figs. 21–25). It also differs from the glyphs of places with related names.

Such places are numerous because of the popularity of the name *tollan*, derived from the combination of two Nahuatl words, *tollan* (or tule), meaning "marsh grass," and *lan*, meaning "place where something exists" (Smith 1973, 70). In the glyphs of many of the *tollans*, "places of the marsh," are literal representations of a particular marsh grass, or sedge, a type often called bulrush, or, more commonly in England, a cattail, because of its brown, cylindrical inflorescence. In the new variant, Tulancingo, are two more Nahuatl words: *tzin*, a reverential and affectionate diminutive, and *co*, meaning in or at (Smith 1973, 70). So the name of our town translates literally as "at the small place of marsh grass," or perhaps more freely as "at the dear place of marsh grass." But there is no cattail on Ihuitlan's lienzo. Instead, the town's distinguishing attribute is the lively flow of water that gave Caso the idea for the provisional name "Agua."

Figure 3 shows how literally the attribute is presented. As if the watery forms of the representations were insufficient, the artist indicated currents by wavy lines, and drew six shells—also signs of water—at the ends of the visible splashing offshoots. There may also have been another shell in the space which is now a ragged hole. Note the two rulers facing each other on what looks like a shelf jutting from the glyph. Their shelf is covered with a tailed jaguar skin. The man sits on a throne with a high back, and the woman's hair is braided. Because their calendrical names are given, they can be identified as Lord 6 Rain and Lady 10 Flint.

They can be named with certainty—and their names understood—because of the naming system the Mixtecs worked out in pre-Conquest times, used in their pictorial documents they created for themselves, and continued to use in documents for the Spaniards. Utilizing their calendar, the Mixtecs named each other after the days on which they were born. They had cycles of twenty days, each with a distinctive sign, and Figure 4 gives a representative set of the twenty Mixtec day signs abstracted from *Codex Nuttall*. It will elucidate not only how the names of this man and woman were derived, but how the names were deduced for other personages with roles to play in our story.

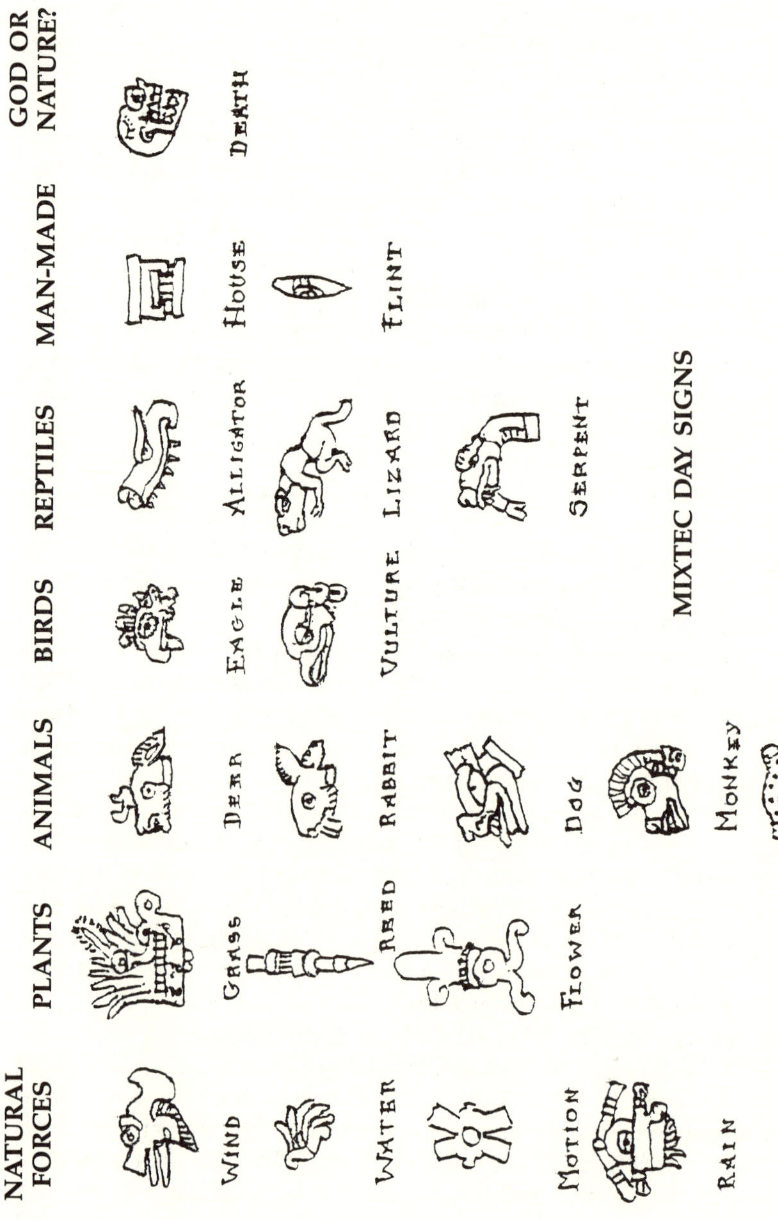

NATURAL FORCES	PLANTS	ANIMALS	BIRDS	REPTILES	MAN-MADE	GOD OR NATURE?
WIND	GRASS	DEER	EAGLE	ALLIGATOR	HOUSE	DEATH
WATER	REED	RABBIT	VULTURE	LIZARD	FLINT	
MOTION	FLOWER	DOG		SERPENT		
RAIN		MONKEY				
		JAGUAR				

MIXTEC DAY SIGNS

FIGURE 4. The twenty day signs of the Mixtec calendar, selected from Codex Nuttall. Rearranged and redrawn by the author.

Figure 4, however, does not present the day signs in their fixed cyclic sequence, but in columns classifying them by the orders which inspired them: the forces of nature, followed by plants, animals, birds and reptiles. Perhaps I should explain why I have named the lowest head in the animal column "Jaguar." Most English-speaking commentators have called this day sign "Tiger." They have taken their cue from "tigre," the word the Spaniards applied when they encountered the New World's largest and most powerful felines. These mighty cats were marked with spots surrounded by circles, rather than striped, but Spaniards, who had never seen them in the Old World, called them *tigres* because they seemed to resemble the tigers of Asia. As the codices and lienzos show, however, it was the jaguar who inspired this calendrical sign. The antiquity of the signs—their antedating high cultural levels—is suggested by how only two, House and Flint Knife, are derived from objects of human manufacture; although one of the plants, Reed, is depicted as man converted it into the shaft for an arrow.

Because the goggle-eyed, long-toothed sign accompanying the ruler in Figure 3 can be recognized as the sign for the Rain God in Figure 4, it is established that the lord's name was Rain, and by counting his dots we know he was 6 Rain. The dots, or little circles, enlarge the calendar's naming capacity because names were increased by supplementing their symbols with units from a thirteen-number cycle. The woman's sign, the day sign for Flint, accompanied by ten dots, shows she was 10 Flint.

The depiction of dates is another writing practice Mixtecs used in their pre-Columbian pictorial manuscripts that they continued in the lienzos they created for the Spaniards. They turned to their calendar for signs for years, as well as for days. But they did not invent new signs for years; the repertory of day signs was treasury enough. Four of the day signs could be converted into year symbols by being integrated into a compound figure like an upper case A stepping through an upper case O. Flint, House, Reed and Rabbit were the day signs elected to double as year signs. Figure 3 gives an example of a Flint year, represented by an A/O pierced by a two-pointed flint knife as conventionalized in Figure 4. The reader, keeping the A/O in mind, can use the day signs for year recognitions, as well as for names. The system is refined enough to pinpoint days as well as years. This is seen when day signs converted by the A/O into year signs adjoin unmodified day signs. Put more simply, when two day signs are shown, one part of an A/O, a specific day in a cited year is indicated.

How can one be sure Figure 3 represents Tulancingo? The proof lies in a photograph that Jesús Franco Carrasco sent me in November 1974. It is reproduced in Figure 5, and shows at the upper level the same rulers, Lord 6 Rain and Lady 10 Flint, seated in front of a temple or palace under which water flows and eddies in a manner reminiscent of the water in the glyph on *Ihuitlan*. In Figure 3 the temple is on a higher level, with two crowned men sitting before it. The ruling couple face each other lower down. In Figure 5 the lord and lady are turned right, with the woman behind the man. Time's passage has rendered both almost faceless, and

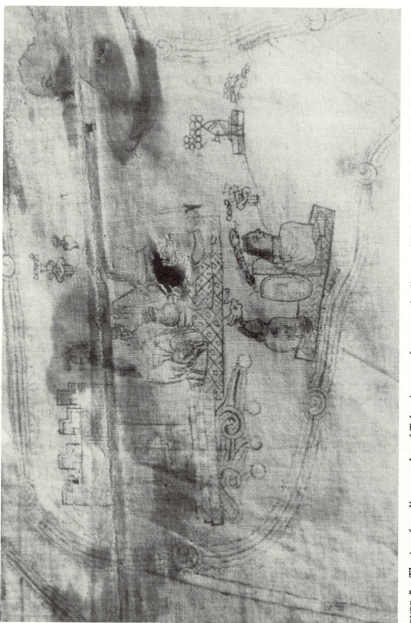

FIGURE 5. The two founding couples of Tulancingo as shown on the lienzo of Tulancingo. Photograph by Jesús Franco Carrasco.

most of the man's body is gone because of a hole, but he is made more individual by being given a personal name, "Heart." The jar between them, and what rises from it, are other additional elements. A smaller couple sits below them. And the rocky place on *Ihuitlan*, shaped like a kettle drum, is missing. So there are differences, but the resemblances are striking, especially when one knows where the photograph was taken.

Franco was a hydraulic engineer who, while working for the Comisión del Papaloapan, visited San Miguel Tulancingo many times. He heard the town had a lienzo, but it was kept secret. Only later, after he had won local confidence, did the men of the *municipio* show him their lienzo, allow him to photograph it, and cooperate in the picture-taking. The photograph, one of seven in color he sent me, was taken in Tulancingo. Figure 5, which is crucial to our identification, shows a detail of the central area near the top of the lienzo. It reveals that the glyph of Tulancingo appears on the town's prize document. It also reveals the position on which the glyph is presented. Both gave me considerable satisfaction. As early as February 1962 when, besides *Ihuitlan*, I knew the four valley sheets, "Antonio de Leon" (*Tlapiltepec*), Seler II, *Coixtlahuaca* ("Ixtlan"), and "Meixuiero," I was aware that Tulancingo was on all five, except *Ihuitlan*. What is more, it was important on them. Why, I wondered, wasn't it on *Ihuitlan* too? By all odds, it should have been. They were from the same valley. It was a mystery to me for more than ten years; now it is resolved. Tulancingo *is* on Ihuitlan's lienzo. It simply was not recognized.

When Engineer Franco sent me his photographs, I had met his brother, José Luis Franco Carrasco, an epigrapher, but not him. The transmittal came about as an outgrowth of my hunting for lienzos of the Coixtlahuaca Valley that began in 1960. That first year I was particularly eager to find the originals of the lienzos that William Gates called "Ixtlan" and "Meixueiro" when he published versions of them in 1931 (Gates 1931a and 1931b). "Ixtlan" proved easy. In the town hall of Coixtlahuaca I recognized a photograph of the sheet on which "Ixtlan" was based. Town officials told me the original was in the Museo Nacional in Mexico City. "Meixueiro," however, was more elusive. I did not have luck with it in 1961 either, even though I showed a copy of it in Suchixtlahuaca, Tequixtepec, Tepelmeme, Ihuitlan Plumas, Tlacotepec Plumas and Tlapiltepec, hoping it might be recognized so villagers could tell me where the original was.

By this time I was familiar with the whereabouts of the originals of the other known lienzos of the valley. Santa María Nativitas still had its lienzo. The lienzo of Ihuitlan Plumas had been in Brooklyn since 1941. A many-named lienzo that Caso called "Antonio de León, to honor a Mexican hero, was in the Royal Ontario Museum in Toronto (Caso 1961, 247). And a second lienzo from Coixtlahuaca, called Seler II because it was obtained by the German Mexicanist, Eduard Seler, was in the Museum für Völkerkunde in Berlin. So the hunt seemed to narrow to the whereabouts of the original of "Meixueiro." A break came in 1963 when Martha Robertson discovered the painstaking tracings from which Gates worked. The tracings had been drawn, probably in the 1890s, by the eminent

Mexican ethnohistorian, Nicolás León, and were in the Latin American Library of Tulane University (Parmenter 1970). The one from which Gates created "Ixtlan" was catalogued as Lienzo B; the source of "Meixueiro" as Lienzo A. In giving us Lienzo A this brought a document closer to "Meixueiro's" original, but not the original itself.

The continuing search led to other unexpected discoveries. One in 1970 was that San Miguel Tequixtepec did not have "Meixueiro," the possibility suggested by a rumor, but it had two previously unknown lienzos of its own (Parmenter 1982, 45–62). Another discovery, in 1973, brought an interplay of geography and history when I found proof that "Antonio de León" came from San Mateo Tlapiltepec (Jansen 1978, 13–16; Parmenter 1982).

Hunting lienzos involved meeting delightful experts along the way, including Mary Elizabeth Smith, then professor of art history at the University of New Mexico, and Irmgard Weitlaner Johnson, the textile expert of Coyoacán. Engineer Franco, a friend of Mrs. Johnson, told her about the lienzo he had photographed at Tulancingo. Because Mrs. Johnson knew Dr. Smith was a specialist in Oaxaca pictorial manuscripts, she told her about it in 1974. Generously, Betsy, knowing my special interest in documents of the Coixtlahuaca Valley, and that Tulancingo was there, told me of Engineer Franco's discovery. At last, it seemed, the original of "Meixueiro" had come to the surface. To check, I sent Franco a photograph of "Meixueiro," and asked if his discovery was its original. It wasn't. The lienzo he had photographed was unknown to any of us, and he sent me his photographs so I could get an idea of the lienzo for myself. At the same time he gave me permission to publish the photographs with an account of the lienzo, provided I gave him the credit for taking the pictures and being the first to tell scholars of the lienzo's existence.

Naturally, I wanted to see the lienzo for myself, and I conceived a plan. Franco was unhappy about how Tulancingo was keeping the lienzo—folded in a glass cabinet in its City Hall. He knew it would be less likely to deteriorate if it was protected in a cedar box, and he planned to have one made for the town. Perhaps, I thought, when he took the box to Tulancingo he might take me with him and introduce me as a friend. It would have been tactless and foolish to try to see the lienzo except under the right circumstances. So I remained patient. In the meantime, unfortunately, a quarrel developed between Franco and the town. Nine years elapsed until someone else stirred me to any action.

This friend was Dr. Nancy Troike of Austin, Texas, another expert on Mixtec manuscripts. In 1983 she planned to rent a car to visit the valley of Coixtlahuaca. Her invitation to go with her gave me the opportunity to visit the town. Nancy agreed that without an ally in Tulancingo's administration, we should first sound out the town's attitude to strangers before asking about its lienzo. Asking to see its church, we felt, would give us our clue as to how far to go in our questioning. That was the year a number of churches in the Mixteca Alta were robbed of important Spanish colonial paintings, so Tulancingo viewed us with understandable suspicion. As we paused for a soft drink, two, and then a third town official materialized. We could not photograph even the exterior of the church, they said. We took the hint, and drove away. Shortly after this I met an official of the Oaxaca state government who frequently visited Tulancingo. He acknowledged the town had reverted to secrecy about its lienzo. Never had he been given a sign of its having one.

Wanting to get on the record the information I had gathered on the lienzo, I wrote the first draft of this study. The next year, 1985, I sought comments on it from Engineer Franco, Dr. Smith, Mrs. Johnson, Dr. Troike, John Paddock, Maarten Jansen, Elizabeth Boone, and Cecil Welte—all friends and all experts in related fields. But I pledged them to silence about Tulancingo's lienzo. I was eager to give Franco the credit he was due, but I was reluctant to reveal the town's secret. All kept honorably quiet, and I made no attempt to get the study published.

I did not need to be so scrupulous. The year before my draft, without my knowing of the disclosure, the secret had already been revealed by a native of the town, Raul Nieto Angel in his *Tulancingo, Oaxaca*, published in November 1984 by the Universidad Autónoma Chapingo. Nieto, in his 80-page monograph, after naming sites near Tulancingo with archaeological ruins, included a paragraph, which, when translated into English reads:

The inhabitants of San Miguel also have the fortune of conserving a Codex of the Colonial epoch, elaborated with the techniques and the style of its prehispanic culture; it is kept in the archive of the municipal president, and depicts Tulancingo in the center, the towns nearby and the roads that lead to them.

Nieto published no photos of the document, and his skimpy account did not suggest the codex was a painting on a sheet, but it alerted scholars to something important. I still did not realize, however, the essential secret was out. Franco died three years after Nieto's booklet appeared. By 1988 I had lost my qualms about guarding what I still thought was a secret. So I planned, finally, to give news of the lienzo to the International Congress of Americanists in Amsterdam. I was looking forward to doing so as a memorial to Franco, especially since thanking and crediting him enabled me, in telling how the news of the lienzo was discovered, I could also thank Mrs. Johnson and Dr. Smith, and introduce most of the other documents pertinent to the discussion. I looked forward, too, for some personal credit for presenting Franco's discovery to a wider audience. But Dr. Troike's Amsterdam symposium, where I wanted to give my paper, didn't materialize, so I decided to save my disclosure on the lienzo's existence for the next Congress of Americanists in New Orleans in 1991.

In the summer of 1989, a new friend, the Colombian ecologist, Carlos Rincón Mautner, who had been visiting the Coixtlahuaca Valley for seven years, made another visit to the region. I told him that Tulancingo had a lienzo, but I warned him its authorities might be evasive and secretive. He convinced them of the sincerity of his concern for the rural development of the area, however, and he showed how he had interwoven information to construct the histories of other communities. They were eager to learn as much of their own history as possible. So they agreed to cooperate with him in photographing and studying their lienzo as part of their own effort to reconstruct their history. This gave him material he did not want to withhold for two years in deference to my wish to have priority in telling the Americanists about the Tulancingo lienzo. So we worked out a compromise. Instead of waiting two more years, I would describe the lienzo briefly at the annual meeting of the American Society of Ethno-historians in Chicago in November 1989. This I did in a symposium organized by Dr. Troike.

Figure 2 is a version of the map I gave out at the meeting. The numbers at six of the places on it were part of my exposition. Besides wanting to show where Tulancingo was, and citing its lienzo as a ninth from the Valley of Coixtlahuaca, I wanted to show where the eight lienzos I knew about earlier originated. A few pages back I listed where they are now—Brooklyn, Toronto, Berlin etc. My map numbers account for the provenance of all nine. As well as those from Ihuitlan and Tlapiltepec, three came from Coixtlahuaca, or very close to it. Two are still in Tequixtepec. And Nativitas and Tulancingo have also kept their lienzos. In contrast to many other pictorial manuscripts from Mexico, the introduction of these lienzos to the public has been slow. Not until 1913 was a fairly comprehensive description of one of them published for the first time, along with thirteen details (Rickards 1913, 47–57). Details from other Coixtlahuaca lienzos have been published since, but over wide intervals, and clear, good scale reproductions of most of them still need to be done. In my earliest paper on them (1961), I may have been the first to list six of them as the nucleus of a corpus of related documents (Parmenter, 1961, Smith 1974, 182).

THE LIENZO OF TULANCINGO DESCRIBED

Four of Franco's photographs give glimpses of the hands and legs of the men who stood behind the lienzo as they held it outstretched for the picture. By providing a human scale, these glimpses show the sheet is a good seven feet high, by five wide—too tall for the men to hold upright. But they understood it could be photographed sideways, and studied in correct orientation if the photograph was placed with the narrow right side at the top. Because to take the lienzo in its entirety Franco had to step further back, his photograph with the total view (Fig. 6) is less clear than the others. Nevertheless one can see that the lienzo's central feature is a big Christian church, bracketed by two bifurcated rivers. Around the church, scattered in no immediately discernible order, are couples drawn in the traditional style of pre-Columbian codices. The sheet is now sand-colored, disfigured in places by rusty stains, so the general impression is of a work in sepia. But the rivers are markedly blue; the roads Nieto said were radiating from the church are white, and a faded rose frame separates a border of place glyphs from the images in the main area of interest.

All these features are indicated in sharp summary in the schematic sketch of the lienzo that Franco made for his own satisfaction and sent me as an aid for my study (Fig. 7). The eight or nine place glyphs outside the frame are suggested by rough sketches of seven of them. Churches, seven in all, are symbolized by crosses, roads by broken lines. Six roads, as indicated by footprints, lead to the small churches: four at the top outside the rose frame, and one on each side just inside the frame. What look like beehives are Franco's shorthand for seated personages. He found nine of the ten couples on the lienzo: the two shown at the top in Figure 5, and the others below and on either side of the dominant church. He also noticed which couples were seated at palaces, which on the woven palm mats known as *petates*. Those on the mats he underscored with single lines. The five at palaces, obviously the more important couples, he distinguished by heavy black lines rising perpendicularly from their underlines. These palaces, decorated on their outer walls as well as their roofs, are ornamented in a similar manner to the largest and most sumptuous palace—that of Lord 6 Rain "Heart."

Like most of the Coixtlahuaca Valley's other lienzos, *Tulancingo* is a map as well as a genealogy. Recognizing that it was not oriented like modern maps with north at the top, Franco indicated that north was on the lienzo's right. Because the western boundary of the valley is along the Continental Divide, with the highest section at Monte Verde in the south (Fig. 2), its rivers run north-eastward. The rivers on the lienzo,

13

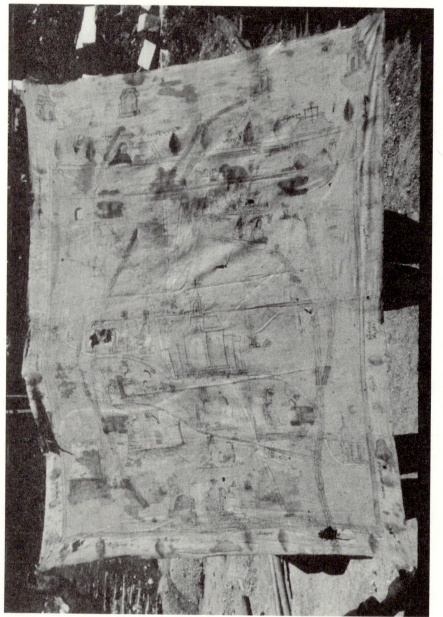

FIGURE 6. The lienzo of San Miguel Tulancingo. Photographed by Jesús Franco Carrasco.

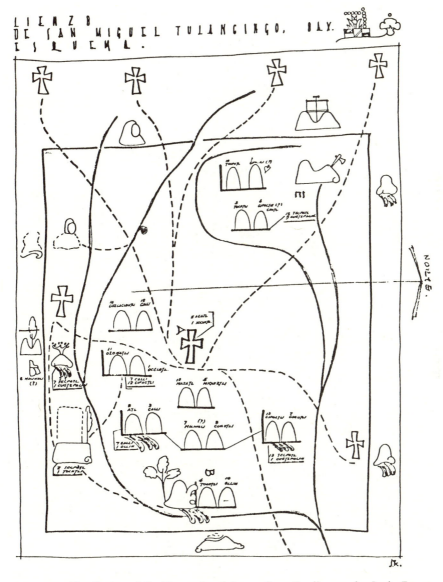

FIGURE 7. The lienzo of Ihuitlan reduced to a schematic diagram by Jesús Franco Carrasco.

FIGURE 8. The Christian church in the center of Tulancingo.

then, only conform to the rivers of the valley if the lienzo is turned upside down and angled to the right—that is, set diamond-wise, with the corner where the augmented rivers run together pointing north. Then their courses approximate reality, and show how intervening ridges hold the rivers in distinctive streambeds. In that position there are two other touches of realism. The starting points of the four rivers, indicated by terminal water spirals, are all in the heights of the Continental Divide; and the correct direction of their flow towards the Gulf of Mexico is depicted by the spirals along their courses. The corner of the lienzo where the main streams converge represents where the valley's rivers join to form the River Xiquila.

The commanding position of the largest Christian church, and the European manner in which the church is drawn (Fig. 8), give proof that Nieto was correct in calling the lienzo "Colonial." In fact, the realistic way in which the church is depicted shows that the sheet was painted long after the coming of the Spaniards. Other indications that it was created late in the sixteenth century are the plump bordering cypress trees, also echoing a European style, the dates, which lack the Mixtec year denominator of an A stepping through an O, and the way women are drawn. All the women on *Ihuitlan* are armless, like Lady 10 Flint in Figure 3.

But the women on *Tulancingo* resemble the two in Figure 5. They have natural-looking arms encased in ample sleeves, and their hands seem demurely clasped in their laps. They are not as anatomically correct as they first appear, however. Their torsos are frontal, but their double-backed legs are in profile, and it is on their thighs that their hands rest. It is worth noting that this is the manner in which seated women are shown on Codex Tulane. There is a further striking likeness to Tulane in Tulancingo's Reed and Flower day signs. They are eccentric on both documents—that is, unlike most representations of them on other Mixtec pictorials—yet they are alike in their eccentricity.

By peering at the sections of *Tulancingo* in Franco's photographs that concentrated on limited areas, and by supplementing them with Rincón Mautner's photos, I could discern most elements on the lienzo (though some not very clearly). But I could not make sense of them all. Like most lienzos of the valley, it told its story in sketchy form, omitting elements too familiar to inhabitants of Tulancingo to need inclusion; nor did the images shown have to be explained or interpreted. But I wasn't daunted. The lienzos of the valley cover so much common ground with supporting information, in varying degrees of completeness, that I was sure I could get close to the mysteries of *Tulancingo* from other sheets.

The twenty persons on *Tulancingo*, as revealed by those already shown, are named, like people on other lienzos, in the pre-Columbian manner, with their day signs accompanied by little circles indicating numbers. Obviously, then, the first approach, and the most likely to be fruitful, was to see if I could find more Tulancingo personages on other lienzos of the valley.

RELATIONS WITH IHUITLAN

The big lienzo of Tequixtepec (Parmenter 1982) was the first I examined; it was the easiest to understand. Thanks to Emily Rabin's careful tabulating of all the figures on it, I could quickly see if it held any of the *Tulancingo* figures. It did not. Not having methodical records of all the people on *Tlapiltepec* and Seler II, I could not search these lienzos thoroughly, but both showed Tulancingo conspicuously. In each case the town was surrounded by named personages (Figs. 24 and 25). To my surprise, none of those named was on the lienzo of Tulancingo. Only after I left Oaxaca and got back to New York did I have success. There I had access to the index cards I had made, one for each of the 190 personages on *Ihuitlan*. Not only did I find seven of the ten Tulancingo couples were on *Ihuitlan*, but the cards showed where I could find four of the couples on *Tlapiltepec*. Ihuitlan and Tlapiltepec, then, must have been towns closely related to Tulancingo, for both recorded Tulancingo history on their lienzos. From the way the lienzos of Ihuitlan and Tlapiltepec structured their rulers, I foresaw they could enable me to determine the correct order of the couples on *Tulancingo*.

The couples on *Ihuitlan* and *Tlapiltepec* are neatly stacked, with each couple placed above the other, and I knew they were to be read upwards. These columns of paired men and women have customarily been referred to as genealogies. The term, however, is only roughly accurate, for, although in most cases sons succeed fathers, and therefore genealogies are represented, succession is not always directly patrilineal. When a brother succeeds a brother, for example, two couples will be shown, but they will be members of the same generation. Sometimes, too, an outsider will inherit the rulership by marrying a daughter. Because of these irregularities in succession, some investigators have begun calling these Pre-Columbian "genealogies" king-lists, including Nigel Davies (1977). But David H. Kelley has suggested[1] "ruler lists," instead—the term I prefer. But what to call the jurisdictions that are inherited? They have been called kingdoms, principalities, city states, and even village-states because some were so small. I used to call them baronies, but, sticking with the suggestion of feudal estates, I now prefer fiefs. Baronies imply the overlordship of a king, and a distinctive feature of these Mixtec jurisdictions was that seldom was there a ruler controlling a sufficient number of fiefs for a long enough time to be described accurately as a king.

Having properly assembled ruler lists to assist in ordering the scat-

---

[1] Personal communication, 14 December 1983.

19

tered *Tulancingo* personages, I knew what to do next. These Tulancingo people were probably rulers too, and how they were related chronologically ought to be revealed by the mutually supporting, trustworthy order of the ruler lists on *Ihuitlan* and *Tlapiltepec*. Accordingly, I decided to establish columns for the three versions of the same ruler list. I would place the short, early ruler list provided by *Tlapiltepec* on the left, and the long, much more complete ruler list given by *Ihuitlan* on the right. With the guidance of these, I would be able to plot the chronological positions of the *Tulancingo* personages on an intermediate column. The results are shown in Figure 9.

One fact is immediately apparent. Although *Tulancingo*, as one would expect, recorded rulers of its village, it did not record them nearly as fully as did the allied town of Ihuitlan. And I quickly discovered that, having a list of extraordinary completeness on *Ihuitlan*, I had a master list that threw light on the two shorter ones. It had the further advantage of illuminating two Tulancingo periods, for two of the lienzos pointed to some kind of cut off with the reign of Lord 10 Motion married to Lady 4 Rabbit.

Early Tulancingo, the years before 10 Motion took control, should be discussed first. We start with 6 Rain married to 10 Flint, the founding man and woman we know through finding them photographed on *Tulancingo*, (Fig. 5) after seeing them redrawn from *Ihuitlan* (Fig. 3). Moving the eye from this couple, across the columns from left to right, we have three lower lines to peruse. There are gaps in each, but the repeated

Rulers of San Miguel Tulancingo on Three Lienzos

Tlapiltepec			Tulancingo			Ihuitlan			
						♂ 1	Vulture	♀ 8	Deer
						♂ 6	Flint	♀ 10	Flower
			♂ 13	Deer	♀ 4	Death	♂ 13 Deer	♀ 4	Death
			♂	*	♀ 3	Eagle	♂ 3 Wind	♀ 3	Eagle
			♂ 4	Water	♀ 3	House	♂ 4 Water	♀ 3	House
						♂ 7	Reed	♀ 3	Motion
						♂ 6	Eagle	♀ 12	Flower
						♂ 4	Eagle	♀ 7	Lizard
						♂ 8	Water	♀ 4	Water
						♂ 10	Rabbit	♀ 5	Grass
						♂ 6	Grass	♀ 10	Serpent
						♂ 12	Motion	♀ 6	Wind
♂ 10 Motion	♀ 4	Rabbit	♂ 10 Motion	♀ 4	Rabbit	♂ 10 Motion	♀ 4	Rabbit
						♂ 6	Motion	♀ 1	Monkey
♂ 6 Rain	♀ 10	Flint	♂ 6 Rain	♀ 10	Flint	♂ 6 Rain	♀ 10	Flint
♂ 4 Rain	♀ 3	Grass	♂ 4 Rain	♀ 3	Rabbit**	♂ 4 ***	♀ 3	Grass
♂ 6 Grass	♀ 2	Motion	♂ 6 Grass ♀ 2 Motion			♂ 6 Grass	♀ 2	Motion
♂ 13 Vulture	♀ 8	Death				♂ 13 Vulture	♀ 8	Death

* Illegible in photo
** Because the rabbit head has 3 ears it may be a mistaken version of grass
*** Day sign lost because of hole in cloth

FIGURE 9.   **The rulers of Tulancingo as given by the lienzos of *Tlapiltepec*, *Tulancingo*, and *Ihuitlan*.**

personages show that, despite what might be a painting error and a loss from a hole in the cloth, three generations of rulers are involved, with the same names in each case. And note that only the *Ihuitlan* list includes the couple above 6 Rain and 10 Flint. What, one wonders, became of 6 Motion married to 1 Monkey, consigned to oblivion by two of the lists? Perhaps this 6 Motion, the son of 6 Rain "Heart," did not live long enough to count in the Tulancingo dynasty. But he and his wife had some importance. Footsteps show (Fig. 10) they provided royal children for two other towns: the son, 12 Alligator, who married 12 Rabbit at the unnamed place in the lower left corner of *Ihuitlan*; and the daughter, 9 Wind who married 11 Deer, the first ruler of Ihuitlan. That there are no further rulers in the left column is easy to explain. It only contains the rulers of Ihuitlan shown on *Tlapiltepec*, and does not pretend to show Tulancingo's rulers.

The anomaly of Ihuitlan's lienzo having more Tulancingo rulers on it than that town's own sheet might be accounted for by the different periods at which the lienzos were painted. Memories of forebears were likely to have been dimmer in Tulancingo in the several decades later when its lienzo was commissioned. When the earlier *Ihuitlan* was painted, however, memories were probably keener, not only of Ihuitlan's own rulers, but of other towns in the valley, also.

On the other hand, *Tulancingo's* omissions might have been deliberate. Perhaps those who commissioned it knew which rulers they wanted to memorialize. By the same token, they may have known which they wanted to dismiss. The seven rulers of what might be called the fief's middle period were possibly not considered worth bothering about.

Next, the lists show that, if the towns of Ihuitlan and Tulancingo were not joined in a single community in their first decades, they had common rulers. Whether originally a single town or two towns with joint rulers, they obviously had close relations with Tlapiltepec, a town situated between them. On the lienzo of Tlapiltepec, Ihuitlan is depicted with its early rulers, the ones shared with Tulancingo. On the lienzo of Tulancingo, a secondary glyph of Tlapiltepec, the Eared Hill (Parmenter 1982, 33) is shown as the glyph of the cut-off pair, Lord 10 Motion and Lady 4 Rabbit, the last of the Tulancingo rulers before the seven omitted nonentities. And on the bottom half of the left side of the lienzo of Ihuitlan, Tlapiltepec is shown as a major conquest of Lord 3 Rain, a middle period warrior from Coixtlahuaca (Frontispiece and Fig. 10). Did *Ihuitlan* record this overthrow of Tlapiltepec to deplore or celebrate the fate of a town important in Ihuitlan's history? Either is possible.

While working for the Papaloapam Comisión, Franco was responsible for creating a finely detailed topographical map of the zone from Coixtlahuaca to Nochixtlan, and it was part of his generous helpfulness to send me a copy. It makes the Tulancingo-Tlapiltepec-Ihuitlan axis revealed to the lienzos intelligible. I must admit this axis puzzled me when, before studying the map, I recalled visits to the three towns. Approached by the improved dirt road, Tulancingo seemed to be in its own valley—a prelim-

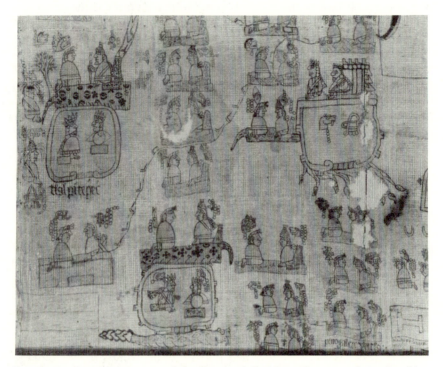

FIGURE 10. Lower left corner of the lienzo of Ihuitlan. (Courtesy of the Brooklyn Museum.)

inary crease in the mountains before the main Coixtlahuaca valley opened to the east. How could it be so politically close to the other towns? The map, based on aerial photographs, showed me. In pre-Conquest days when men traveled only on foot, and even after Spaniards brought the horse, men and women used different routes to get from one place to another. Ñaate, the mountain rising to 2,600 meters between Tulancingo and Tlapiltepec, was a barrier then, as now. But natives of Tulancingo, not needing roads that could be traversed by wheeled vehicles, found a way of skirting the great hill by proceeding north and curving around it to the east. That path, or burro trail (still on the map), while steep, lacks the confusing indirectness of present roads forced to find easier, more level routes. It is probably hardly longer than the seven miles between Tulancingo and Ihuitlan as the crow flies. On this footpath, Tlapiltepec is a way station, being at the two thirds point before reaching Ihuitlan.

By 1960 Caso was pointing out (1960a) how remarkably the Mixtec codices agreed on their historical information. The solitary discrepancy of Lady 3 Grass or Rabbit on these three lienzos illustrates this. It also allows confidence in identifying two other names on the sheets. The late ruler of Tulancingo, marked with an asterisk in Figure 9 because of the illegibility of his name in Franco's photo, was almost certainly 3 Wind

FIGURE 11. The year of the founding of Tulancingo, year 12 Flint, day 5 Serpent, as given on the lienzo of Tulancingo.

because his wife was Lady 3 Eagle, and on *Ihuitlan* 3 Eagle's husband was 3 Wind. And the name of the ruler at the jog in *Ihuitlan*, designated by three asterisks because of a hole in the cloth, was just as surely 4 Rain, because that was the name of the ruler in the same sequence on *Tlapiltepec* and *Tulancingo*, depicted on them too as married to 3 Grass.

Dates as well as names, Caso noted, were generally in agreement on the Mixtec codices; so cross-checking the pictorial manuscripts helps with dates, also. An excellent example is provided by how *Tulancingo* and *Ihuitlan* in combination resolve the puzzle of an important date in Tulancingo's founding. On *Tulancingo* the Mixtec year denominator is missing, but the symbols 12 Flint 5 Serpent (Fig. 11) prove to be a date because of the information on *Ihuitlan* (Fig. 3). In this version the interlaced A/O is present, but the date is incomplete. It gives us a 5 Serpent day, but a hole has taken away the number accompanying the year sign. But the upper point of the flint knife remains, showing it is a Flint year. So we are not at a loss. The consensus of the 5 Serpent day on *Tulancingo* lets us trust its 12 before the Flint. So we can be sure the year was 12 Flint—especially because this makes the year and day signs the same in each date, and we know the date is associated with founding rulers of the same place.

Let us look a little more closely at those founding rulers shown in Figure 5. The larger rulers—Lord 6 Rain "Heart" married to Lady 10 Flint—were identified earlier because they were the same rulers as at the glyph of Tulancingo on *Ihuitlan* (Fig. 3). The smaller couple has also been identified. Here the husband, 4 Rain, has the added personal name of "Serpent," indicated by the snake drawn over his head. Because his lady's day sign looks so much like the head of a rabbit, I have followed Franco in calling her 3 Rabbit. But four things cause doubts. Rabbits don't have three ears, yet this one seems to have three. The rabbit-like sign, perhaps because it was no longer well understood, resembles two other signs on the lienzo that are unmistakably Grass. A proven 4 Rabbit sign has wide ears coming to points. And 4 Rain's wife on *Tlapiltepec* is clearly 3 Grass. Thus she might be Lady 3 Grass. If she is, another discrepancy disappears.

Further attention must be called to the placement of the founding couples in Figure 5. It is near the top of the lienzo, just right of center. And this high position of the couples shows the manner in which Tulancingo's arrangement of its rulers differs from that of most lienzos. How the succession lists of *Tlapiltepec* and *Ihuitlan*, as examples, agree on stating that 6 Rain "Heart" and 4 Rain "Serpent" are early rulers is by following the general post-Conquest custom of presenting founders at the bottom. Yet *Tulancingo* puts these founding rulers *above* the latest ones shown. Occasionally the most important rulers were given emphasis by being given central positions. Yet here the church preempts the center. Deprived of this for their major forebears, the planners of the lienzos apparently thought of an alternate form of emphasis. One might call it the headline treatment. For 6 Rain "Heart" and 10 Flint are depicted as larger types at the top.

The date just confirmed—year 12 Flint, day 5 Serpent—is attached on *Tulancingo* by a fine line to the smaller, lower founding couple (Fig. 5). The attachment on *Ihuitlan* is by the shelf jutting from the kettle-drum shape that frames the date (Fig. 3). Note this *Ihuitlan* attachment is to the upper couple, Lord 6 Rain "Heart" married to Lady 10 Flint. A confusion of claims is indicated as to which couple deserves chief credit for founding the fief. The town historian of Tulancingo or whoever laid out the basic scheme for the artist, apparently arrived at a compromise solution, granting the founding date to the lower couple, but acknowledging *Ihuitlan's* insistence on the greater importance of the upper couple in developing the fief by having the upper couple drawn larger. The disagreement seems to be on emphasis; or, how the credits should be distributed. With agreement on the founding date, on the names and sequence of the founding males and the visual components of the glyph, there can be no further doubt that "Agua" is San Miguel Tulancingo.

Clinching the identification necessitates learning a little of the history of Tulancingo; which, in turn, reveals the fascinating way comparative study of these lienzos fills out knowledge of the area. As lienzos go, *Tulancingo* has only a moderate amount of information; whereas *Ihuitlan* is loaded with it. Yet the limited facts of Tulancingo have already provided a major key to the perplexities of the larger sheet. The big sheet, in turn, has helped fill in gaps in the smaller one, answering some questions and others not asked. Through our comparisons we have also learned how, lacking a written language when they developed their artistic traditions, these people used visual devices, such as joining lines, footprints, placement of material, omissions, unconventional sequences, and the scale of drawing to underline points they wanted to make.

CASO'S WRONG GUESS

Learning from Ihuitlan's lienzo the names of several later rulers of Tulancingo established another important fact: which ruler list close to the glyph of Tulancingo on *Ihuitlan* shows the rulers of Tulancingo. The first detailed description of *Ihuitlan* was published in 1961 with the appearance of Caso's "Los Lienzos Mixtecos de Ihuitlan y Antonio de León." A model of its kind, because it also gave a detailed description of *Tlapiltepec* (Parmenter, 1982), it was a major contribution to knowledge of documents from the Coixtlahuaca Valley. But, unfortunately, he ascribed Tulancingo's ruler list incorrectly, and his choice of the wrong column for Tulancingo also caused a mistake about the alternate ruler list.

The two long columnar lists about which, for want of written identification, Caso had to make decisions are shown on the frontispiece, to the right of the glossed ruler list of Coixtlahuaca. How those equivocal lists begin, if understood, explains the confusion, and those beginning can be seen up close in Figure 10. The first ambiguous ruler list rises directly above 6 Rain "Heart" and Lady 10 Flint, sitting on the shelf jutting from the glyph of Tulancingo. The other ambiguous list rises almost as directly from the two unnamed figures with saw-toothed crowns sitting in front of the temple or palace on top of the glyph. How can one tell which column shows the rulers of Tulancingo? Not having seen the town's guarded lienzo, Caso did not have help in his study, as we do. He had to make a choice that seemed reasonable. He guessed that the list rising above the men with the saw-toothed crowns was the ruler list of Tulancingo, his "Aqua." But when we turn to the frontispiece showing all the successors to the named couple on the shelf (the middle column), we find the eleventh ruler up is 4 Water, who can be seen more easily on Figure 12, second couple, middle column. This 4 Water, as shown in Fig. 9, was a ruler of Tulancingo. We know he is the same 4 Water because he has the same wife, Lady 3 House. Above them are the twelfth rulers of Tulancingo: the woman is Lady 3 Eagle, and the lord, whose name is illegible on *Tulancingo*, must be 3 Wind, for he is shown clearly with that name on *Ihuitlan*. Above them the concordance of rulers is continued, for the thirteenth rulers of Tulancingo are the same pair shown on *Ihuitlan*, Lord 13 Deer, married to Lady 4 Death. That these three couples appear in *Ihuitlan's* list connects that list with the forebears, Lord 6 Rain and 10 Flint, seated on the shelf. The list rising directly above the shelf, therefore, is the ruler list of Tulancingo, not, as Caso stated (1961, 246), the second dynasty of Ihuitlan.

This revelation further underlines that Ihuitlan's list of its neighbor's

FIGURE 12.   Top section of the three long ruler lists on Ihuitlan. Three couples in the middle column, starting with Lord 4 Water, appear also on *Tulancingo*. (Courtesy of the Brooklyn Museum.)

rulers is more complete than Tulancingo's own. By omitting two ruling pairs following Lord 13 Deer, Tulancingo's authorities, apparently, felt it had two more nonentities whose names were not worth preserving. And we have not exhausted all that can be learned when the two Tulancingo ruler lists are compared—the short one on the town's lienzo, and the long, gap-free one on *Ihuitlan*. What must be understood is that the order of Tulancingo rulers in Figure 9's middle column was derived not from Tulancingo's lienzo, but from Ihuitlan's. On its lienzo, Tulancingo's rulers are given in different order. Already it has been said that those clustered around the central church seemed scattered without discernible order; while the point was forcibly made that the town's founding fathers, at the bottom of the list by chronology, was given "headline" placement by being drawn in large scale at the top of the lienzo. Now that we know who Tulancingo's eleventh, twelfth and thirteenth rulers were, we are in a position, by correlation of names, to show the couples below the church are not placed in a haphazard manner after all. Three are segregated to make a point, and there is considerable logic in the placement of the rest. All of this can be followed fairly easily in Franco's diagram (Fig. 7). Although the line of couples under the church wavers, its vertical intention can be distinguished, and the names show the reading should be upward. The couples deliberately out of the plum line (one above the other to the left of the church, and the third near its foundation to the right) seem to be rulers of neighboring towns still to be identified. The other four couples leading up to the church are in the succession of Tulancingo rulers, having the sixth, twelfth, eleventh and thirteenth positions in the *Ihuitlan* list. The rulers in *Ihuitlan's* second position, 6 Grass married to Lady 2 Motion, are also on *Tulancingo*, but far out of line, outside the rose frame, in fact, about a third of the way up on the left. But because the edge of the cotton is so ragged here, Franco caught only 6 Grass's head wearing a half miter crown.

By the nineteenth century Tulancingo and Ihuitlan were in different parishes (Martínez Gracida 1883). Nevertheless, that *Ihuitlan* gave a succession of fifteen Tulancingo rulers shows that, even after they ceased having common lords, Tulancingo and Ihuitlan were important to each other. In later centuries they may have been more important to one another than Coixtlahuaca was to either of them. *Ihuitlan* supports this visually. On the lienzo as the Frontispiece shows, their genealogies are almost touching, whereas the gap between Tulancingo's rulers and Coixtlahuaca's, while small, is noticeably wider. Despite the depiction of Coixtlahuaca on *Ihuitlan* as one of a triumvirate, one searches in vain for any conspicuous sign of Coixtlahuaca on the lienzo of Tulancingo dominated by the central church. Perhaps Tulancingo, having been a subject town of Coixtlahuaca so long, tried to establish its autonomy from its *cabecera*, as Dr. Smith found other Mixtec towns tried to do in the last half of the sixteenth century.

When we look at the placement of the earliest Tulancingo-Ihuitlan rulers on the lienzos (Fig. 10), further information can be gleaned. In showing in Figure 9 a jog at 6 Rain on the *Ihuitlan* list, I have tried to echo this placement above the three earliest rulers on the list (Fig. 10). They are not directly below him and his wife, Lady 10 Flint, on the shelf. They are to the right, with the lowest couple, Lord 13 Vulture and Lady 8 Death, beside a pre-Columbian ball court, indicating it might be ancient Ihuitlan. Under them is the gloss, "pinoyalco yvitla," belonging, apparently, to the place of the ball court. According to Caso (1961, 245), these words could be translated as "where he humbled himself." He called these earliest rulers the first dynasty of Ihuitlan.

Tulancingo is sketchier about these six forebears. Figure 9 shows it omits the earliest couple, 13 Vulture and 8 Death; and, while it includes 6 Grass and his lady, 2 Motion, they are outside the rose boundary (a placement also echoed by a jog.)

Tlapiltepec includes all the forebear rulers with their spouses, but agrees with *Tulancingo*—probably for a common reason—in omitting the fifth couple, Lord 6 Motion and Lady 1 Monkey. And it does not present a break at 6 Rain and 10 Flint. Instead, by placing Lord 10 Motion married to Lady 4 Rabbit at right angles to the main line, it hints the break came after them. Again we may see confused claims for founder credit. And note that the ruler list of *Tulancingo* echoes *Tlapiltepec's* break after 10 Motion and 4 Rabbit. At this point *Tulancingo* starts its omission of the succession of seven rulers who may have been nonentities.

What does one make of this? With further thought, the earlier speculation that Ihuitlan and Tulancingo might once have been two towns with joint rulers seems unlikely. Chiefs of state don't customarily operate out of two capitals, especially through four or five generations. What is more plausible is that after the 80 to 100 years of those generations a single town split into two. But the agreement to separate shows that relations remained amicable, for the new town, besides remaining allied with the old, wanted apparently to preserve in its annals the forebears it formerly shared with the other. Assuming that one fief achieved independence from the other, one asks which was the mother settlement? Here the way Ihuitlan is depicted on *Tlapiltepec* (Fig. 9, left column) gives the answer. It lacks any of Tulancingo's later rulers; so the Tulancingo faction was the group that voted to move south and create an independent town on a different river system.

All three lienzos agree that Tulancingo began with a new set of rulers. As indicated by its jog, *Ihuitlan* gives both the date and the founding glory to 6 Rain. *Tulancingo* gives the credit and the date to 4 Rain, but concedes through his smaller size, that he was not as important as 6 Rain "Heart," his successor. *Tlapiltepec*, because it attributes the five rulers of its list to Ihuitlan, seem to imply that 12 Motion, whom it does not name, was the first independent ruler of Tulancingo. Yet *Tulancingo* omits this ruler. With rulers that far back in time, it is not surprising that there is confusion among the three towns in claims and memories. But in their consensus in omitting 6 Motion, married to Lady 1 Monkey, *Tlapiltepec* and *Tulancingo* agree he was not a key figure.

When I took a large framed photograph of *Ihuitlan* to Santiago Ihuitlan Plumas in 1960, perhaps the most important piece of information the villagers gave me was the pre-Columbian manner in which the original town was depicted on the lienzo. It was not by the Christian church glossed as "Santiago yuitla" (frontispiece)—that was the symbol of the present town—but by the black serpent entering the feathered hill with the axe at its crest (Fig. 13). Caso knew this when he published his *Ihuitlan* study. Even though the tail of this serpent practically touches the first rulers of the third great column upper right corner (Fig. 10), he did not take the hint. He ascribed these rulers to "Agua" (1961, 246), which we now know is incorrect, because "Agua" is Tulancingo, and Tulancingo's rulers form the second column. Instead, those rulers of the third column, as the proximity of the glyph of the serpent, the feathers and the axe suggests, are the rulers of Ihuitlan. Perhaps, to preserve Caso's terminology, they form the second dynasty of Ihuitlan. Starting with Lord 11 Deer married to Lady 9 Wind, this dynasty (Frontispiece) extends through seventeen ruling pairs to the top of the sheet, making it the longest ruler list on the lienzo, and the one at the sheet's center line, which is only proper since it shows the rulers of the town for which the

FIGURE 13. **The glyph of Ihuitlan Plumas on the lienzo of Ihuitlan.**

lienzo was painted. And this provides another nice example of how the creators of the lienzos were skilled in the manipulation of non-verbal visual emphasis.

The closeness of Tulancingo and Ihuitlan, once they were independent, is revealed by the fact that the first lady of the second dynasty of Ihuitlan, Lady 9 Wind, is shown, by a line of footprints, to be the daughter of the nonentity, 6 Motion, the sometimes omitted second ruler of Tulancingo. She gives the first indication of an important fact established by the correct identification of Tulancingo. The many outgoing footprints branching at various points from its married couples show how those couples provided sons or daughters to be rulers or first ladies of other towns in the valley, as well as northern towns outside the valley. In this, Tulancingo easily sets the record. The same couple that gave Lady 9 Wind to Ihuitlan, gave a founding ruler to an unnamed place in the lienzo's lower left corner. And when the other lines of footprints branching from Tulancingo are counted—three on the left and one on the right—it can be estimated that Tulancingo furnished six personages to the ruling lineages of other places. Could Tulancingo blood be prized as evidence of special superiority, as descent from the Toltecs of Tule, Hidalgo, was honored by the Aztecs? Ihuitlan, in contrast, only contributed a single first lady to a neighbor near the end of its long ruler list. And Coixtlahuaca's aristocratic children, it seems, never married into the

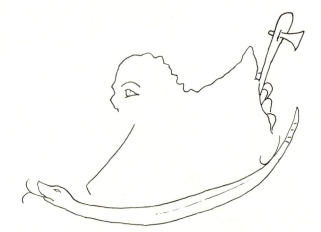

FIGURE 14. The glyph of Ihuitlan Plumas on the lienzo of Tulancingo.

lines of Tulancingo and Ihuitlan, though a man who possibly was one of them, Lord 3 Rain, achieved the throne of Tlapiltepec by both conquering it and marrying its first lady, 6 Deer.

A new look at Figure 5 shows further evidence of the closeness of Tulancingo and Ihuitlan provided by another pictorial element on *Tulancingo*. In the upper right corner is a mountain with a human head, with part of a serpent curving like a rocker at the base. When the view is shifted to embrace the whole glyph, as in Figure 14, it can be recognized readily as the glyph of Ihuitlan, the serpent, the hill and the copperbladed axe forming the components in common. So the top part of Tulancingo's lienzo showing the town's founders also includes the glyph of Ihuitlan. My guess is that Ihuitlan was essential to Tulancingo's founding—as the ruler lists of Figure 9 suggested.

EASTERN AND WESTERN COIXTLAHUACA

At this point, further examination of the Frontispiece is helpful, for the photograph of Ihuitlan's whole lienzo, reduced as it is, shows the layout of the composition, where the details are located in relation to each other, how the three great ruler lists dominate the left half of the sheet, and how Tulancingo couples provide sires and spouses to neighboring fiefs. Now we are in a position to talk geographically, for all three towns contributing the major ruler lists can be located. Coixtlahuaca, long known because of its glossed glyph of a rattlesnake (Fig. 15), is on the left, Tulancingo is next, and Ihuitlan's rulers divide the sheet down the middle. And here it should be said *Ihuitlan* is also a map. It represents a valley running north and south, with confining mountains on the east and west. The rivers are not indicated, and not all the numerous settlements are properly related in space, but when Coixtlahuaca and Tlapiltepec, the glossed towns at the lower left, are coordinated with what we have established as Tulancingo and Ihuitlan, and the four are correlated with their counterparts on a modern map (Fig. 2), we can discern an attempt to establish respective locations, despite the spatial priority given to rulers. We find that there seems to have been a division between the towns of the western side of the Coixtlahuaca valley and those of the eastern.

The big lienzo of Tequixtepec (Parmenter, 1982) proves that this town also had many rulers, descendants of 11 Lizard, whose brother, 3 Lizard is shown on the lower right corner of *Ihuitlan* (Frontispiece). Had 11 Lizard's successors been included, the right half of *Ihuitlan* would have looked very different. And this half would have been crowded had still unknown ruler lists from Tepelmeme, and other eastern towns glossed in *Ihuitlan*, been worked in. The east was not sparsely populated, as the many blank spaces of *Ihuitlan* imply. It is only that in keeping records each side of the valley tended to preserve its own history, and ignore that of the other. That none of the people of *Tulancingo* appears on *Tequixtepec I* provides an example. Even more telling is how *Tequixtepec I* treats the two greatest dynasties shown on *Ihuitlan*, *Tlapiltepec*, Seler II, *Coixtlahuaca* and Lienzo A, the five major documents of the western lords.

Figure 16, drawn from Lienzo A, the nearest document to the original of "Meixueiro," shows descendants of those two dynasties. The one on the left is Lord 4 Jaguar—or 4 Tiger, as he is often called—seated at a temple before a *remolino* ("whirlpool of water"). *Tlapiltepec* and Seler II show he came from Miltepec, a town some distance north of the Coixtlahuaca Valley, but still within the Mixteca Alta. To give him the full name bestowed on him by Caso (1979, 323), he is 4 Tiger II, "Tigre." Caso called

FIGURE 15. The glyph of Coixtlahuaca on the lienzo of Ihuitlan.

him the second to distinguish him from the 4 Jaguar eleventh in the Miltepec line, while 4 Jaguar II is the seventeenth; and Caso derived his personal name, "Tigre," from his wearing the helmet of a jaguar knight. The scion of the other line, seated at the right, is Lord 10 serpent, and his temple is at a place characterized by a round stone with an eye at its center. Both places seem to ride on a feathered serpent suggesting a Viking ship. This is because the places are subdivisions of Coixtlahuaca, established after what seems to have been a conquest, which will be discussed later. Both rulers are late in their lines.

The line of 10 Serpent was founded by a man that *Tlapiltepec* and Lienzo A call 1 Wind, while *Ihuitlan* and Seler II call him 8 Wind, but all four of the lienzos prove him to be the same person citing Lord 5 Flower as his succeeding son, and three of them naming his wife as 4 Reed. (Lienzo A does not show a wife.) When the lords of this line are coordinated, one finds an incredible succession of thirty-one rulers, which might span a period of more than five centuries, or at least three, if ten years are allowed for each reign.

The line of the 4 Jaguars, comparatively, is made up of parvenus. Seler II places 4 Jaguar I as the founder of a new dynasty of only fifteen rulers. *Tlapiltepec* gives him ten reigns of forebears.

Yet how are the lines of these important lords treated on *Tequixtepec I*, the major eastern document? Only the earliest members of 10 Serpent's line are shown, and 4 Jaguar's line is not shown at all. Not enough eastern documents exist to show how many eastern alliances there were. That "Agua," obviously an important town even when unlocated, has

FIGURE 16. Lord 4 Jaguar, left, ruling at Remolino-Coixtlahuaca. He faces Lord 10 Serpent, ruling at Ojo-con piedra-Coixtlahuaca. This is the central drawing of a lost lienzo known in copies as Lienzo A-Meixueiro.

been identified means it is no longer a floating entity that could be one of several places in the valley. It is Tulancingo, and it is in the west. And because Tulancingo has been proven to be so closely associated with Coixtlahuaca and Ihuitlan, we are assured of long-lasting western alliances.

The discovery of Tulancingo's lienzo augments and supports the hypothesis of western alliances in another way, too. Besides letting us know with which allegiances one of the valley's important towns sided—a positive fact—it furnishes a negative one. None of the eastern lords known through the Tequixtepec lienzos is on it. However this is probably not as significant as the paucity of information about the eastern lords on the other western lienzos. One characteristic that sets *Tulancingo* apart from those other western ones is that it is virtually what can be called a one-family sheet. It details a single ruler list, whereas they cover many.

One can see the interplay between geography and history, then, through geographical identification of Caso's "Agua" as Tulancingo leading us this far. Although this identification of another valley glyph has made the history on the Coixtlahuaca lienzos more vivid and these lienzos supplement each other, many ambiguities remain.

The case of Lord 3 Rain is an example. On the frontispiece he can be found ten rulers up from the tail of *Ihuitlan's* black serpent, and he can be seen in larger scale as the third ruler in the right list on Figure 10, where, with his black mask, he suggests a highwayman. We now know he was not a personage from "Agua" (Tulancingo). Being in the Ihuitlan list he was associated with Ihuitlan. His Ihuitlan wife, Lady 6 Monkey, sits back on her heels facing him. When we look at the ruler seated at the outspread, realistically marked jaguar skin at Tlapiltepec (Fig. 17), we see his Tlapiltepec wife is Lady 6 Deer, but that he is the same man who is revealed by the name 6 Monkey, that of his Ihuitlan wife, who, like a ghost, is present in name only. How he gained his position in the Ihuitlan succession is not indicated by any special means, but that he came to the throne of Tlapiltepec by conquest is shown by the war path of inverted chevrons curving down from the eleventh rulers of Coixtlahuaca. His forerunners in each ruler list differ, so he does not seem a son of either preceding couple.

On the lienzo of Tlapiltepec, where Lord 3 Rain is seen with both wives in full body, there are still other forerunners. Whose son was he? Was he born in Ihuitlan, Coixtlahuaca or Tlapiltepec, or was he an interloper from another region, who acquired fiefs both by conquest and by marrying inheriting daughters? We do not know, except that he seems historical when we know the towns in which he held commanding positions. That he conquered five other towns (one probably Tehuacan in the state of Puebla) is proved by lines stretching from him to arrows embedded in neighboring glyphs, an arrow with its point buried in a glyph being the sign of conquest.

FIGURE 17.   Lord 3 Rain ruling at Tlapiltepec after his conquest of it. Lady 6 Deer is his
Tlapiltepec wife; Lady 6 Monkey (shown only by her name) was his wife at Ihuitlan.
Detail from lienzo of Ihuitlan.

THE MEN OF THE SAW-TOOTHED CROWNS

When the glyph of Tulancingo drawn on *Ihuitlan* (Fig. 3), was introduced, passing attention was called to the unnamed figures with saw-toothed crowns sitting in front of the temple on its leveled top. At the opening of the discussion of how Caso came to confuse the rulers of Ihuitlan with those of "Agua," they were used as identifying markers for the ruler list above them. At this point these crowned figures have been seen enough to suggest they deserve recognition because similar figures are conspicuously associated with Coixtlahuaca and Tlapiltepec. The crowns are thought by some to be made of *amate*, a tree bark, while others believe they were woven of cane. Three male couples wearing them can be seen in Figure 10. The pair at Coixtlahuaca have names—1 Lizard and 9 Wind—but those at Tlapiltepec and Tulancingo are nameless. This suggests they are not historical in the same sense as the other personages on the lienzo. Two—the heads balanced on balls—may not even be human beings; and though the rear figure at Tulancingo has a rump to sit on and legs to keep him stable, he seems to be related to the other legless ones by the large disk that obscures most of his cloak.

Might they be legendary founders? Perhaps. But a story told on other pictorial documents of the Coixtlahuaca Valley suggests an alternate interpretation. The story is told most fully on the Selden Roll (Ms. Arch. Selden A.72 (3)), which is in the Bodleian Library in Oxford (Burland, 1955), but it is also seen in various degrees of detail on *Tlapiltepec, Tequixtepec II* (Parmenter 1982) and Seler II. The story, as pieced together from these four documents, is that four chieftains wearing saw-toothed crowns descended from heaven and at a double temple with a ball court they acquired an object precious to them all, a ball surmounted with a head wearing the duck bill mouth mask of the wind god. After this, the four start on a journey, taking the head on the ball with them. On the way they conquer several places. Figure 18, photographed from the Selden Roll and reproduced with the Bodleian Library's permission, shows one of the late scenes in their mission, for so it seems to be. Here one sees they have reached a rock plateau, and their lance-carrying leader, 10 House, is the one toting the sacred head on his back. By the time of the ensuing scene they have reached a high hill enveloped by mighty serpents—a hill I have proposed may be Ñaate (Jansen 1978).

On this hill (as illustrated plentifully in my *Four Lienzos*, but not here) the Wind God head on the ball is set on an altar and before it the crowned men kindle a symbolically important fire. They do it by their leader, 10 House, twirling a spark-producing stick in a log held steadily horizontal

FIGURE 18.   A section of the Selden Roll showing the four chieftains of the new religion near the end of their journey. Of the two places above them, indicated as conquered by the horizontal chevrons, the upper one is certainly Tlapiltepec, the Hill of the Knot, and the lower one with the water swirling under the temple is probably Tulancingo. (Courtesy of the Bodleian Library.)

by two of his fellow missionaries. The ceremony's importance is attested by the presence (especially on Seler II) of rulers from many surrounding towns. Taking his cue from depictions of teams of god-bearers on other codices, Caso interprets the story as an account of the introduction of a new religion into the area, specifically, that of Quetzalcoatl (1954). Because the head installed on top of the hill resembles that of a figure known as Lord 9 Wind, often taken to be Quetzalcoatl, Caso's interpretation is widely accepted.

The name of the straw-crowned head venerated at Coixtlahuaca (Fig. 10) supports Caso's thesis about this particular valley. The head lacks Quetzalcoatl's customary mouth mask, but it has Quetzalcoatl's name—9 Wind.

The balls surmounted by heads at Tulancingo on *Ihuitlan*, then, may well be representations of the new god—idols, as unbelievers would say. The men with similar crowns attending the idols may be priests dedicated to the new cult. This might also explain four other men on *Ihuitlan* with saw-toothed crowns. Seen at the bottom of Figure 19, they are at the mid-latitude of the sheet, to the right of center. They suggest priests even more strongly than the lower figures, for their faces, like those of the original idol-bearing chieftains, are painted black. That they are not the chieftains who brought the image of Quetzalcoatl to the valley is shown by their different names. The place they face is a square hill with the day sign 6 Motion. It is surmounted by a temple in whose vestibule one sees a digging stick leaning against a bell-shaped object that Caso interpreted first (1961, 247) as a tied bundle and later (1979, 357) as a loin cloth. The place is not glossed. Above them rises a column of eight paired rulers, which reaches a temple-crowned hill glossed as Texcalhueyac, which Caso interpreted as "despeñadero," (precipice from which rocks fall). Though he favored this upper place, Caso did not decide with certainty whether this ruler list belonged to the glyph at the bottom or near the top. His dilemma can be readily understood by puzzling over Fig. 19 reproducing *Ihuitlan's* upper right corner.

The place in question was obviously important, not only because of the four crowned figures, but because this ruler list—though shorter than those of Coixtlahuaca, Tulancingo and Ihuitlan—is longer than that of any other on the lienzo. It is, then, the lienzo's fourth most important place. Though *Tulancingo* cannot give such decisive help with this community as it did with "Agua," short of certain identification, it tells us much about what I am going to call Place Q—largely because this is shorter and easier to remember than the Temple of the Digging Stick and the Loin Cloth. Besides, this provisional name might be apt, not only because Q stands for question, but because the place gives indications of being associated with Quetzalcoatl.

The first fact *Tulancingo* gives is that Place Q was founded by a scion, not of Ihuitlan, as Caso implied, but of Tulancingo, a town committed to the religion of the men of the saw-toothed crowns. His name was 6 Serpent, and the evidence that he was the son of a Tulancingo lord is

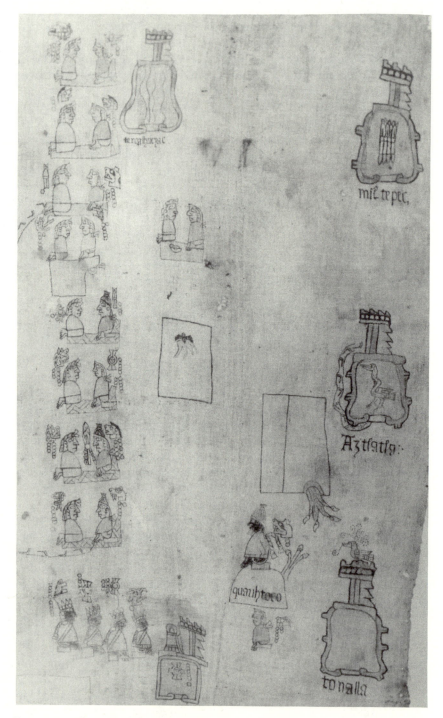

FIGURE 19. The upper left corner of the lienzo of Ihuitlan, showing its fourth most
important town, provisionally named Place Q.

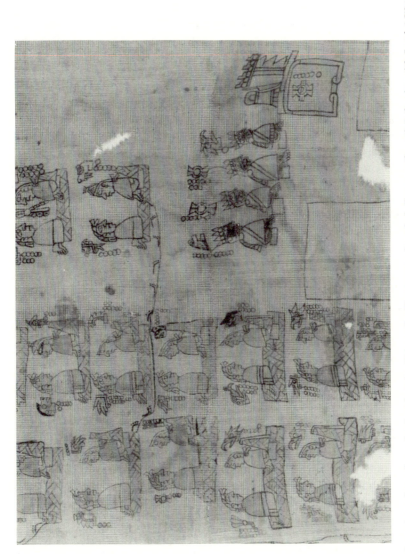

FIGURE 20. The line of footprints shows how the fourth ruler list on the lienzo was founded. Because the prints begin with Lord 4 Water on the left and proceed to Lord 6 Serpent on the right, one can see that Lord 6 Serpent, the ruler-founder of Q, is a son of Lord 4 Water and Lady 3 House, the eleventh rulers of Tulancingo.

given in Figure 20 by the footprints leading to him from 4 Water, the eleventh lord of Tulancingo. He and his wife, 5 Alligator, are one couple below on the right, and the line to the straw mat on which they sit, by going to his feet (and not hers), shows that he was a Tulancingo son, while she was a daughter from some other place. The connecting line allows one to count the footsteps leading from father to son. There are eight. Lord 4 Water, as Figure 9 has shown, was a ruler of Tulancingo who reappeared on the lienzo of his town after a succession of seven unnamed nonentities. Perhaps it was siring the ruler of an important new place that warranted his being returned to town favor by being named among its rulers. Besides showing who 6 Serpent's parents were, those eight footsteps show that Place Q was near Tulancingo. That they indicate a short distance is proved by the long lines of many footsteps shown elsewhere on *Ihuitlan* between places that positive identification has revealed were truly distant from the three main towns.

The nearness of Place Q to the core towns is proved by another line of footsteps. This one, on Figure 12 top right, consisting of six prints, shows that the sixth first lady of Place Q, Lady 1 Reed, was the daughter of a ruler of Ihuitlan, specifically, Lord 5 Death, the husband of 5 Wind, a step below her on the left. This intermarriage between a ruler of Place Q and a daughter of the rulers of Ihuitlan shows further that Place Q, besides being within the Valley of Coixtlahuaca, was a member of the western alliance.

If *Tulancingo* indicates that Place Q was a town founded some ten generations later than Tulancingo and belonged to the western alliance, it also gives us strong reasons for discarding the possibility of Texcalhueyac being the town of the fourth ruler list on *Ihuitlan*. Texcalhueyac may never have been in Coixtlahuaca's central valley, or it may have been a town that has disappeared without trace. No settlement of that name, or even a close approximation to it, appears in *Gazetteer No. 15, Mexico, Official Standard Names*, issued by the United States Board of Geographic Names. Nor does Texcalhueyac appear in the extensive listing of places in Peter Gerhard's *A Guide to the Historical Geography of New Spain*. Carlos Rincón Mautner, who found evidence of ancient settlements lost when amalgamated with surviving ones, has found nothing convincing on Texcalhueyac, though he thinks it could be a version of Atexcal, a town listed by Gerhard in the district of Tepeji de la Seda in Puebla. Whether Texcalhueyac still exists or not, the implications of *Ihuitlan* show that it is north of the Valley of Coixtlahuaca, for it is at the top of the lienzo, shown to be farther north than Miltepec, which is definitely outside the valley, and almost as far north as Tehuacan, which is in the state of Puebla. Again look at *Ihuitlan* as a map, Place Q is somewhat north of Ihuitlan, but it is not far enough north, to be Texcalhueyac. Besides the rulers of place Q nearest to the glyph of Texcalhueyac do not touch the glyph, as do the couples associated with subsidiary places on the lienzo. Furthermore, the fewness of the rulers associated with those subsidiary places shows that it is not *Ihuitlan's* way to give genealogies of peripheral places.

Nor is it in keeping with the character of the lienzos of the Coixtlahuaca Valley to place identifying glyphs at the top of the ruler list. The convention is to place them at the bottom, with the lineages ascending.

If Place Q is not Texcalhueyac, which of the places in the valley is it? Caso did not find identifying aid in the other known lienzos of the valley, for he did not find Q's eight ruling couples on any other pictorial manuscripts. We need therefore to discover another lienzo, lost or held in secret, or some other document giving early town rulers with calendrical names, to make the correct attribution. Meanwhile, because *Ihuitlan* gives us Place Q's approximate location, north and a little east of Ihuitlan, a hint or two might be gained from a modern map like Figure 2. There Concepción Buenavista appears as the most likely prospect. But the present town is not Place Q. As its Spanish name reveals, this town is a Spanish creation that does not go back to pre-Columbian times. Concepción Buenavista, however, is at the foot of a hill that is dramatically surmounted by a steep, spired mesa, suggestive of desert forms in Arizona. Could the chapel known as Torrecilla perched on the mesa's tip have superseded an ancient site that might be Q? Another contender, almost as geographically plausible, is a place with the exciting name of Veinte Idolos, which implies pre-Columbian ruins. Volume V of Martínez Gracida's *Los Indios Oaqueños y sus Monumentos Arquelogicos* shows in its plates 68 and 69 that the Hill of Twenty Idols has the ruins of a fortress and a temple. Perhaps they might be the remains of Place Q. Veinte Idolos is not on my map (Fig. 2), because I never found it on a map of the region, and no native ever located it satisfactorily for me. Nicholas Johnson in his extensive explorations of the valley in the summer of 1992, however, learned that it was almost outside the valley in the north, 17 kilometers northwest of Concepción Buenavista, and almost 12.5 kms. directly west of Aztatla.

Whatever its ancient name, or its present identification, Place Q, as depicted on the lienzo of Ihuitlan, seems to have a double character: secular because of the eight ruling couples rising above it, and religious because of the four crowned men, whom Caso agrees are priests. The day sign within the frame of the glyph, 6 Motion, he thinks could be either the name of the deity or the overlord of the place (Caso, 1961, 247). My supposition is that the presence of so many priests at the one temple suggests an important shrine to the new god introduced by the chieftains wearing similar crowns, perhaps a place of pilgrimage. Place Q is therefore the fourth place in the valley where the new religion took root so strongly that they became principal cult centers. It may or may not be significant that they all seem to be in the lands of the western alliance.

Because of their glosses, Tlapiltepec and Coixtlahuaca were the first such cult centers in the valley uncovered by modern decipherers. Ihuitlan, because of Caso's wrong guess, seemed to be the third. With the correct identification of "Agua," we know that Tulancingo, not Ihuitlan, was the third cult center for Quetzalcoatl. It is not surprising that a place founded by a scion of Tulancingo should be a fourth one.

As established, the glyph of Tulancingo on *Ihuitlan* (Fig. 3) and *Tulancingo* (Fig. 5) has a temple with water swirling swiftly under it from the left. This glyph suggests that Tulancingo is also represented on the Selden Roll. Look at the place just above the men with the saw-toothed crowns (Figure 18). Unfortunately no named rulers or date make the identification irrefutable, but that glyph, with the six drops of water at the ends of the splashing offshoots of the river flowing under the temple base, closely resembles the glyph of Tulancingo we have been considering. Also the Selden Roll's origin in this western division of the valley, and its heavy emphasis on the establishment of the new religion, make it likely that Tulancingo, so important to that religion, would appear on the Roll. The line of chevrons leading to it shows it was conquered, or perhaps converted. Note the glyph of the other conquered place higher up on Figure 18—the hill with the knot on top. That is Tlapiltepec, another town of the valley associated with the religion of the men with the saw-toothed crowns.

THE CATTAIL GLYPHS

In referring to Figures 24 and 25 on page 5 I may have caused confusion. I showed a glyph in those illustrations which had a cattail as a leading element, and said it represented Tulancingo. How could this be if *Tulancingo*, *Ihuitlan* and probably the Selden Roll showed Tulancingo's glyph is a palace or temple under which water flowed? This inconsistency brings us to the four lienzos of the valley whose glyphs were said to differ from the palace-water ones in the discussion of the English translation of the name Tulancingo. Their cattails are their major elements of difference. As a prelude to consideration of why the glyphs differ, it should be noted that the running water glyph consorts more fittingly with the present town of San Miguel Tulancingo than does any glyph featuring a cattail. Tulancingo is in a valley so steeply sided that it has been called a "rocky gorge" (Martínez Gracida 1883). The east side, perhaps because it has been terraced for agricultural purposes, now seems to slope upward in shelves, but the west side sweeps up precipitously to a chain of high hills dominated by one called El Anillo. The defile, or preliminary crease as I called it, slants sharply, causing Agua Dulce, its river, to run swiftly. It also runs musically, for the town is blessed with plentiful water originating in the western hills that tower over it. A lively flow of water, then, is characteristic of the village. It is what one might expect on its glyph. But there is no place for water to settle into ponds or swamps, where cattails and other sedges generally flourish. So the cattail on the glyph is topographically anomalous. Perhaps settlers from some other place, when they migrated, brought it with them as a symbol of an ancestral home they had left.

A topographical feature that might properly have appeared on the glyph is the largest of the ahuehuete trees that grow along Agua Dulce. Trees of this species (*Taxodium mucronatum*), related to the cypresses of Louisiana's bayous, are often called tules, with the most famous being the tree of Santa Maria del Tule near Oaxaca. Some people in Tulancingo believe the name of their town derives from the largest of their tules. But this is unlikely when the other plant called a tule—the cattail—appears so often in one of its glyphs, and one finds no indication of a giant tree like an ahuehuete associated with the glyph of the temple and the running water.

Of the four cattail glyphs of Tulancingo on Coixtlahuaca documents, the one with the least information is on Lienzo A (Fig. 21). It consists of a steep flight of steps, with a cattail standing, as if rooted, on the platform at the head of the stairs. Because of the balustrades and a top tier with an ornamented frieze, the building suggests a platform to support

FIGURE 21. **The glyph of Tulancingo as shown on** *Lienzo A*, **the simplest of the representations of the cattail glyph.**

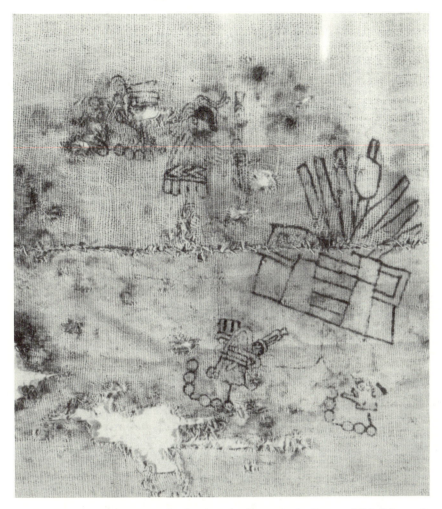

FIGURE 22. The cattail glyph of Tulancingo as shown on the lienzo of Coixtlahuaca in the Museo Nacional of Mexico.

a temple, resembling the base of many pyramid-temples in early pictorial manuscripts. But there is no temple. Could the ceremonies here have all been performed in the open air? A hole encroaching on the bulrush has taken away whatever information, if any, might have been there. But the date below is unharmed. It is the year 6 Reed, day 6 Dog.

On *Coixtlahuaca* (Fig. 22)[2] the stem of the cattail does not rise so high, the plant is larger in proportion to the platform, and the chunkier platform recalls many exposed by excavations at sites from which crowning

[2] José de Jesús Reyes, photographer for Mexico's National Museum, took this photograph for me at the request of Yolanda Mercader, director of the museum's library. My thanks to them both.

FIGURE 23.   The cattail glyph of Tulancingo as shown on Lienzo B in the Latin American
Library of Tulane University. Xerox, taken from the tracing, courtesy of Tulane.

temples have disappeared. However the correspondences between the
glyphs are clear. Potentially the painting in this photograph (Fig. 22) has
more to tell us than the Lienzo A version because of additional information supplied by the personage on the left. As can be seen, he is a man
waring a black mask, holding an arrow pointed down. Because of two
holes where his name is given, the nearest Caso could come to his name
was "12 (?) Lluvia (?)" (Caso 1977, 129).

Fortunately there was a means of getting a more accurate reading of
his name—Lienzo B that Martha Robertson had discovered in the Latin
American Library of Tulane University. Before *Coixtlahuaca* was acquired
by Mexico's National Museum the lienzo had been used as a horse
blanket (Parmenter 1970, 189). Lienzo B, León's tracing of it on which
Gates based his "Ixtlan," had been drawn before it was so shamefully
used. The likelihood was that the original then had fewer holes worn in
it. So I asked Martha for a xerox copy of the section of the tracing showing
Tulancingo. She sent me Figure 23. My hunch was vindicated. The holes
that frustrated Caso's reading were not present when León did his
tracing. Besides seeing the man's advanced leg more clearly, León could

see that eight (rather than a possible twelve) was the full complement of dots accompanying the man's day sign. Further, he could see the beard in the day sign, revealing that the horizontal projections above the beard were not water jets (as in the sign for water) but elements in the duck bill mouth mask in the sign for Wind (Fig. 4). So the personage associated importantly with Tulancingo was 8 Wind.

This was an identity worth going after. For 8 Wind's inverted arrow associates him with other rulers on the Coixtlahuaca's lienzos, and he is almost certainly the 1/8 Wind shown by four lienzos as holding a pivotal place in the longest and greatest of the valley's lineages. His presence here is a link between historical events in the valley reflected in *Tlapiltepec* and Seler II, specifically the transactions at the cattail temple platform to be discussed below. Despite his lost presence on *Coixtlahuaca* retrieved by Lienzo B, Lord 8 Wind is not on the lienzo of Tulancingo.

Note that the date accompanying the glyph of Tulancingo on *Coixtlahuaca* is the same as the accompanying date on Lienzo A, and that it is year 6 Reed, day 6 Dog is even more unmistakable on the original lienzo than on the tracing.

Before speculating about this date common to Lienzo A and *Coixtlahuaca*, the much more elaborate glyphs of Tulancingo on *Tlapiltepec* and Seler II deserve a closer look.

The platform with the cattail at the head of the steps and the same date—year 6 Reed, day 6 Dog—appears again on the glyph of Tulancingo on *Tlapiltepec* (Fig. 24). But here there is more. Two posts rise on either side of the bulrush. Each supports a thick cord adorned with what suggests a large, eight-petaled artificial flower. In front, a little to the left, and at right angles to the platform, is a place obviously related to the platform by more than proximity, for a cattail rises up its back like a spine. Seated on the hassock-like jaguar throne, with the jaguar's tail curving up at the back, is a ruler with arms determinedly crossed at his chest. Unfortunately, a hole has taken away the sign of his day, so we do not know his name. Caso thought he might be the same man shown near Tulancingo on *Coixtlahuaca* (whose name also seemed to be lost). Thanks to León's tracing, we know that man was 8 Wind. If Caso's idea about the two men being the same personage is correct, this man is 8 Wind too, and the eight incontrovertible dots of his name that survive form the full complement.

Because of the objects drawn, Case named the place *Tula Templo, con cuerdas con rosetas* (1979, 113). Clearly he felt it safer to make up a name from the visual elements than to opt for a specific place which might turn out to be a mistake. In his day the big open question was: could this glyph represent Tula, Hidalgo, the place which Wigberto Jiménez Moreno, in one of the landmark linkages of geography and history in Mexican studies, identified as the legendary Tollan, the home of the Toltecs, from whom any later tribes claimed they were descended (Jiménez Moreno 1941, 79–83). Jiménez made the connection in 1939 and Jorge Acosta's excavations the next year proved he was right. That this

FIGURE 24. **The cattail glyph of Tulancingo as shown with an accompanying scene on the lienzo of Tlapiltepec.**

place of the cattail might be Tula, Hildalgo, even though it appeared on a Oaxaca document, was plausible because some Mixtecs were among those claiming Toltec ancestry.

The glyph of Tulancingo on *Tlapiltepec* differs in more than having a large number of pictorial elements. Here there is not only a glyph; there is a scene in which something is happening. To the right are six figures, all named and probably all in religious service, for the upper two, classed as acolytes by Caso, are painted black, and the other four are wearing black dotted garments which Caso recognized as the *xicolli* worn by priests. The occasion recorded, then, might have been a religious conference. Or did the priests come as petitioners, seeking some favor? Whatever the motive of their visit, it is likely that they came in the year 6 Reed, day 6 Dog. This still does not tell us which year this was in the Christian calendar, but at least it gives us clues why this date also accompanies the simpler, undramatized Tulancingo glyphs on Lienzo A and *Coixtlahuaca*.

The names of the six priests can be read in Figure 24. Because we are shortly to meet four of them again, the names of this quartet will be translated into words. The topmost pair on the right, believed to be acolytes, are 1 Vulture and 2 Water. The leader of the threesome facing the ruler is 12 Reed. Behind him is 12 Death. Does the lienzo of Tlapiltepec show where they came from? It does, for Caso's sharp eyes distinguished among the many footprints and paths on the sheet a track of footsteps coming from a place to which he gave the provisional name *Rio de la*

Palma, for it shows a palm tree growing on an island in a water-filled bowl-shape, a frequent indicator of rivers (1979, 228).

The scene at River of the Palm Tree is not illustrated here, but two of its participants play a part in our story. It shows its lord, named 1 Wind, rather than 8, seated in front of a palace or temple, who, because he holds a bow and arrow, looks more warlike than the lord of Tulancingo. One of his attendants carries a bow and arrow, which led Caso to believe these two men might be Chichimecas, for these northern people used bows, whereas the more southern people catapulted their equivalents of arrows (short lances) with throwing sticks known as *atlatls*. The attendant with the bow is 4 Jaguar II, seen in Figure 16 as the lord of the place with the whirlpool behind its temple, so we know that he was an important conqueror who founded a dynasty at a sub-division of Coixtlahuaca. The other attendant who will be met again is 12 Water.

The glyph of Tulancingo on Seler II (Fig. 25) is still more elaborate. Elements common to *Tlapiltepec*, however, are instantly recognizable, notably the front view of a platform, with steep steps, two slender posts supporting ropes, and the large flowers Caso called rosettes. Here, in place of a cattail at the head of the steps is what Carlos Rincón Mautner plausibly interprets as a sacrificial stone, but cattails grow on each side of the platform. And one sees the same date, year 6 Reed, day 6 Dog. There is no cattail palace with a lost-named lord sitting before it, but there may be its equivalent. One question to be asked is what is represented by the parallel vertical lines that run at right angles to the steps of the platform? When the glyph is turned sideways, despite the horseshoe shaped hole, one can see that these parallel lines also represent the steps of a balustraded platform. This second platform seems to overlap the base of the principal one. Surely this presents a miscalculation, an idea supported by plants seeming to sprout horizontally from the second platform's balustrade. Ink drawing on cotton is almost impossible to wash out, and two theories are plausible. Either the artist planned to orient the Tulancingo temple platform across the sheet and then thought better of the idea when it was too late to eliminate the false start; or he wanted to present two temple platforms at right angles on two sides of a patio and found he had not allowed space enough for both platforms and the scene of the visiting priests. So he made the best of a bad bargain by drawing images that overlapped. Bolstering this supposition is the profile figure in the balustrade of the plants. The plant before his nose could easily be a bough supported in an undrawn right hand. If so, he echoes, in reverse, the man offering him a bough, 12 Death, who leads the threesome approaching him. The way his left arm bends upwards behind him supports this view by echoing the upraised hand of Lord 12 Death.

The location of this personage in relation to the platform steps and his appearing to be a host suggest he might be the lord long lost by name from *Tlapiltepec* (Fig. 24)—or perhaps the 8 Wind with the black mask of Lienzo B (Fig. 23). Because his name was extremely difficult to read, I

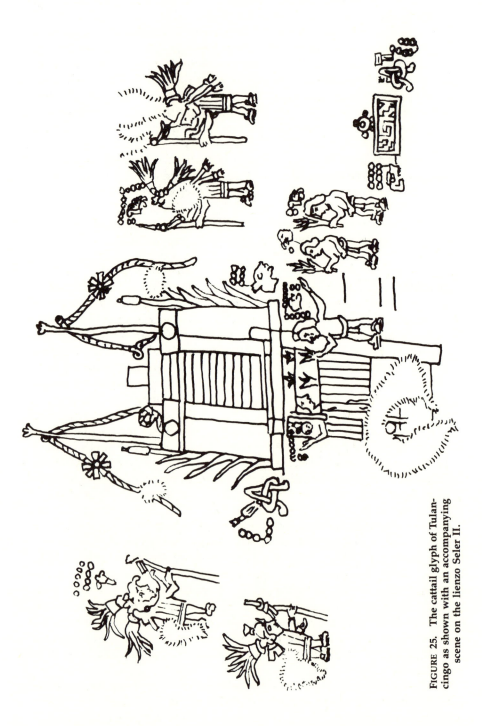

FIGURE 25. The cattail glyph of Tulancingo as shown with an accompanying
scene on the lienzo Seler II.

sought help. The best the Hamburg group[3] could make of it when examining the enormous Seler II in Berlin was Lord 11 or 12 Lizard (Koenig, n.d.). Because this seemed hardly justified, I turned to Nick Johnson, who had access to better photos of Seler II than I did. Through his sharp eyes and sketching skill, he convinced me the man was 12 Reed, almost obliterated by being under the later drawing of the lesser stairway. This confirmed that Caso (1979, 312) was right in interpreting him as the leader of the four priests and two acolytes coming to Tulancingo on *Tlapiltepec*. This ruled out my speculations that the identity of the almost hidden personage might have solved the mysteries of two other figures.

As a source of a scene of action, the Seler II version is also more elaborate than the *Tlapiltepec* version, but we can discern its scene is closely related. All four of the priests of *Tlapiltepec* reappear here, with three seeming to bear tribute boughs to 12 Reed, their leader on *Tlapiltepec*. And the absence of the two acolytes—1 Vulture and 2 Water—is offset by additional personages; four great warriors with elaborate quetzal feather headdresses—two with double feather clusters in their headdresses, two with single clusters. The first lord on the right with the double headdress is Lord 12 Water, one of the attendants at the River of the Palm Tree from where the priests came.

Supplementing this information on how 12 Water and 4 Jaguar II appear on other lienzos of the Coixtlahuaca Valley, Caso (1977, 133) worked out an ingenious explanation of the Tulancingo scenes. In 1265 Coixtlahuaca was conquered by lords from other places who founded four new fiefs which he named from the pictorial elements in their glyphs. In Figure 16 attention has been called to one—*Remolino-Coixtlahuaca*, designated thus because of the whirlpool behind the temple ruled by 4 Jaguar II. The same illustration shows a second, named *Piedra con ojo-Coixtlahuaca* from the "stone with eye" behind its ruler, Lord 10 Serpent, the descendant of 1/8 Wind's great line. What Caso argues (1977, 129–131) is that the predatory lords, 4 Jaguar II and 12 Water, sought the aid of Chichimecas at Palm Tree River, and then, accompanied by supporting priests, proceeded to Tulancingo to win sanction and blessing for their proposed conquest of Coixtlahuaca. That the blessing solicited for the war was granted might be indicated by priest 12 Reed turning to face his colleagues.

Because of the heart included in its glyph, Caso called the third new fief *Cerro del Corazón-Coixtlahuaca*, and for the spurting blood in the glyph of the fourth fief, Caso named it *Cerro de la sangre—Coixtlahuaca*. The number of different Coixtlahuaca may explain why there are so many

---

[3] This group, directed by Berthold Riese, worked under the auspices of the Arbeitstelle für Amerikanische Sprachen und Kulturen der Universität, Hamburg, and presented its detailed study of *Seler II* at the International Congress of Americanists in Paris in 1976. Its members were Viola König, Manfred Kudlek, Marie-Luise Heimann, Gloria Laria Lara-Pinto and Peter Tschohl.

lienzos from this particular valley. Many feudal lords had to explain their respective claims.

I have included the Place of the Jewel at the lower right of the Tulancingo scene on Seler II (Figure 25), not only because it is part of the composition, but because Lienzo A and *Tlapiltepec* also show a place with a jewel close to Tulancingo. On Lienzo A it is located prominently above Tulancingo, with the jewel on top of a platform with lofty steps, and has the date 6 Rabbit, day 5 Vulture. On Seler II the date is 7 House, day 6 Serpent. On *Tlapiltepec* the jewel is within a temple part way up a hill, and there is no date.

Further to the left of *Tlapiltepec* is a second place with a conspicuous jewel. Here the jewel is inset within a hill that looks like a sugar loaf, which has a fret across its feet. This place is dated 10 House, day 8 Serpent. Because its days are the same, and the House year varies by only three digits—10 instead of 7—Caso (1979, 254) accepts it as the place on Seler II shown in Figure 25. But it may not be. *Tlapiltepec's* place with the jewel inset in the hill has been securely identified with Tejupan, a town at the start of one of the major passes to the Valley of Coixtlahuaca. *Tlapiltepec*, then, shows that Tulancingo had close relations with Tejupan. In his excellent M.A. thesis, Nick Johnson (44–45) suggests a resolution for the puzzle of more than one jewelled place. If the glyph of the jewel in the sugar loaf form is accepted as representing Tejupan, that place could be thought of as Jewel Hill. This would enable us to use the provisional name of Jewel House to distinguish it from the glyph without a hill top seen on Seler II, Lienzo A and *Tlapiltepec*. If this is likely, Jewel House was an important place in the valley, which, like Texcalhueyac in the north, seems to have disappeared.

VALLEY GENERALIZATIONS

Before examining the puzzling differences between the two glyphs of Tulancingo—the one with the running water and no cattail, and the one with the cattail and no river—a few generalizations about the lords of the Coixtlahuaca Valley may be helpful. Fortunately, we have a good description by a Latin American historian greatly interested in the state of Oaxaca, William B. Taylor. In "Landed society in New Spain: View from the South" (*Hispanic American Historical Review*, [1974]: 407) Taylor has a summary from non-pictorial documents which agrees remarkably with the impressions furnished by the lienzos. It makes all the more impact because Taylor was not aware how the pictorial manuscripts told the same story.

After discussing political systems in the north of Mexico, he wrote:

By contrast, in southern Mesoamerica there were no native states or cities in the postclassic period comparable to the Aztecs and Tenochtitlan-Tlaltelolco. There were small regional states or clusters of communities under one set of political leaders, but the basic unit of Indian society in the south was the local community. Regional market places were important meeting places for the exchange of goods among communities, but they did not give rise to comparable political and social ties.

This strength of the local community and what seems to have been a state of chronic warfare in the postclassic period of Indian prehistory prompted an exclusivist, suspicious posture toward the outside and coherent, cohesive attitudes within. Such a localized, enemy-oriented political and social system was both a weakness and a strength for the community. On the negative side, it prevented a united front against Spanish penetration, prompted violent discord among communities, and enabled the Spaniards to "divide and rule"; but the same values and cohesiveness also served the communities well in resisting outside encroachments and in maintaining the lands that supported their local society. Spanish rule in southern Mexico was always more remote and more limited than in central Mexico, not only because there were fewer Spaniards but also because the new lords could not simply replace an existing state with an established tradition of centralized control at the local level as they could in the center of Aztec sovereignty.

Battles between peoples even within so limited an area as the Coixtlahuaca Valley illustrates Taylor's words about chronic warfare. The careful maintaining of records of rulers over several centuries shows the cohesiveness of the fiefs. And the creation of the lienzos to prove to the Spaniards how the regional lords deserved their holdings demonstrates the strong impulse to preserve their lands after Spanish rule began. Thus Taylor's words illuminate the Coixtlahuaca Valley, as well as other southern regions.

Around 1445 a lord of Coixtlahuaca, Atonaltzin, who boasted of descent from the Toltecs, managed to bring many fiefs together under his command to alter somewhat the pattern in his valley. This unification made Coixtlahuaca a tempting plum for the Aztecs. Because Aztec traders came there to buy and sell, they knew Coixtlahuaca was not only rich in itself, but commanded passes to the rich Pacific coast.

By this time, the Aztecs, under Itzcoatl, the fourth in a well-documented list of Aztec rulers, had defeated the Tepanecas, ruling at Azcapotzalco. In throwing off the yoke of Azcapotzalco, the Aztecs had become not only independent, but the leading power in the Valley of Mexico. Moctezuma Ilhuicamina, more easily remembered as Montezuma the Elder, succeeded Itzcoatl to the throne of Tenochtitlan in 1440, and he began the first great drive to transform the Aztec domain into an empire. Barbro Dahlgren, author of a primary study, *La Mixteca: Su Cultura e Historia Prehispánic*, believes that the first Montezuma sought a pretext to conquer Coixtlahuaca. Such a conquest, besides bringing him the town's wealth and opening his way to the Pacific, would eliminate Coixtlahuaca as a commercial rival to Tenochtitlan. Atonaltzin was rash enough to give the Aztec ruler the pretext he sought. Some Aztec traders passing through Atonaltzin's territory, it seems, were arrogant and discourteous, and were murdered for their rudeness. According to the *Anales de Cuauhtitlan*, Montezuma launched an attack on Coixtlahuaca to avenge the killings. Atonaltzin fought off the first attack, but could not sustain the second, and, according to one story, he was killed by his own feudatories. Various dates—1453, 1458, 1461 and 1464—are given for his downfall. One of Montezuma's prizes, according to a romantic account, was Atonaltzin's beautiful wife, Lady 7 Serpent. The conquest enabled the Aztecs to control the Valley of Coixtlahuaca for the next three generations; an occupation confirmed by the archaeological evidence that Ignacio Bernal found when he excavated across the river from the town of Coixtlahuaca in 1948.

Aztec expansion continued under later rulers. Ahuizotl, the eighth, who governed from 1486 to 1502, was the next to engage in widespread conquest, and he made deep incursions into the Mixteca and through Zapotec territory beyond, reaching as far as Tehuantepec. One finds the names of many places in Oaxaca, too, among those subdued by Montezuma II, who was next in succession. But the number of Mixtec and Zapotec places Ahuitzotl and Montezuma II actually conquered by military force is problematic. Some, no doubt, were actually attacked, but few, it seems, were held for long. In most cases the fear of being conquered was a strong enough incentive for the majority of Oaxaca towns who became tributaries to the Aztecs to agree to pay heavily for the privilege of being left politically independent.

That the Aztecs considered Coixtlahuaca, the prize they had won from Atonaltzin, the most important center in the Mixteca is shown by page 43 of the *Codex Mendoza*, part of which is a copy commissioned by Viceroy Antonio de Mendoza of the *Matricula de tributos*, a register believed to have been compiled for the younger Montezuma around 1512 to provide himself with knowledge about the tribute his subject towns were obligated to pay. Mendoza wanted a version of the *Matricula* to give Carlos V a concrete idea of how wealthy Mexico was when it was incorporated into Carlos's empire. This page 43 is the only one of *Mendoza* devoted to tribute paid by Mixtec communities. In addition to Coixtlahuaca at the top of the list, it names ten others, all outside the Coixtlahuaca Valley, including Yanhuitlan, Teposcolula, Tejupan and Cuicatlan.

Another scholar on whose work one can build is the late John McAndrew, who made a careful study of the records of Coixtlahuaca, his main interest being the church, the open chapel, and the monastery—all magnificent in scale—that the Dominicans completed in Coixtlahuaca in the 1580s. In his *Open-Air Churches of Sixteenth-Century Mexico*, he cites many facts about the Coixtlahuaca Valley, which, in the light of how shrunken, impoverished, isolated and ignored by historians Coixtlahuaca has been, are hard to credit, except by those familiar with its lienzos.

One can assume that the many feudal lords in the area were attended by a large number of servants and serfs. Thus the lienzos, with their many ruler lists, make it relatively easy to accept the notion that the now sparsely populated area was once, as McAndrew states, populous. Indeed, when you see how crowded with people the lienzos are, and remember how the valley can be traversed on foot in a day, it is easy to imagine how dense the population must have been. And McAndrew supports the idea of its immense prosperity—that it might indeed have seemed a serious commercial rival to Tenochtitlan—by the statistics he drew from page 43 of *Codex Mendoza*.

Coixtlahuaca was probably the collection agency for the Aztecs for all the tribute from itself, the towns of its valley, and the other ten communities shown by their glyphs on the page. The glosses with the glyphs show that Coixtlahuaca by itself did not contribute all that largesse. The page does not specify, however, what share each community was apportioned to provide. In saying that it was all paid by Coixtlahuaca and calling Coixtlahuaca a "kingdom"—and perhaps somewhat misleadingly naming it the capital of the Mixtec kingdom—McAndrew implies an exaggerated idea of what Coixtlahuaca's resources could offer. Besides producing everything to sustain its large population, including those who lived in kingly style, Coixtlahuaca and the other towns forwarded to Montezuma more cochineal than all other towns in his empire combined that produced the rich red dye. Every six months it sent 1,200 shirts, 400 blouses and 400 loin cloths. Annually it sent many gourdsful of gold dust. Mistakenly, McAndrew said twenty-five when the codex cited twenty, but he estimated the gold tribute still exceeded that of any other tribute-paying center. Besides sending 800 bundles of quetzal feathers, Coixtlahuaca annually sent three banners and two shields, with the fronts of these war items adorned with striking designs achieved by hundreds of tiny bright feathers serving for pigments. The feathers would come from Ihuitlan, whose Nahuatl name, "place of feathers" was underlined when the Spaniards added *plumas*, their word for feathers, to the town's pre-Conquest name. And Ihuitlan, with one of Mexico's great feather markets, provides one example of the Coixtlahuaca Valley's having one of the regional market places of southern Mexico that Taylor cited. Tropical birds are not native to the mountain heights above the valley, so those sold in great quantities in Ihuitlan must have been brought there from other areas.

McAndrew discovered something further about Coixtlahuaca. To understand why the Dominicans built so sumptuously there, he lined up the major religious and administrative centers in Mesoamerica, and came up with the following as preeminent: Tenochtitlan, Tlaxcala, Texcoco, Tzintzuntzan, Cholula and *Coixtlahuaca* (italics mine). Thus what the lienzos suggest through their depiction of the arrival of the chieftains and the new religion they established is confirmed by other sources. Coixtlahuaca was a major religious center in pre-Conquest Mexico. Christianity, therefore, if it was to supplant the old religion, was obligated to build splendidly there to counteract the memory of a powerful religious establishment. That McAndrew did not include the Zapotec Monte Alban indicates that he was aware that this site had diminished in power by the eleventh century. The non-inclusion of Tlaxiaco, Tilantongo, and Achiutla shows, too, that these other Mixtec centers, important as they were, stood lower in the religious scale than Coixtlahuaca. That they also had lesser economic importance is indicated by the fact that they were not among the ten subsidiary Mixtec towns paying tribute to Montezuma.

When Coixtlahuaca's eminence in population, wealth and religion is appreciated, the extraordinary number of fine sixteenth-century lienzos produced in the valley is perhaps not so surprising, especially because, as Taylor pointed out, there were few Spaniards in the south and they were thus particularly dependent on local Indian nobles to maintain peace and order—which they did in return for guarantees of continuance in their feudal lands and privileges.

Why, then, did the once rich Coixtlahuaca decline so incredibly? McAndrew suggests that in the first century of the Conquest, it suffered, as did other regions of heavy indigenous population, from the ravages of diseases introduced from Europe. Because Cortés's forces took Coixtlahuaca in 1520 before the conquest of Tenochtitlan was complete, Coixtlahuaca perhaps did not escape the smallpox that broke out as the Aztec capital was under siege. It certainly did not escape the plague of 1544–46, which may have killed as many as 1,000,000 throughout Mexico—as McAndrew cites, more than any disaster in Europe since the Black Death. Worse yet was the outbreak of *cocolixtli* in 1575, which rose to "a horrible climax" the following year and did not abate until 1579, with about 2,000,000 deaths in one year. The Mixteca was specifically devastated by a pestilence in 1591–92. Nevertheless, because of cochineal, and silk-raising introduced by the Spaniards, Coixtlahuaca's population did not diminish as much as many other towns in that plague-ridden century. But Coixtlahuaca's veins of gold were shallow and soon gave out.

What really brought "the death blow" was the drastic dwindling of the valley's water resources toward the end of the Colonial period. Tulancingo shared in the valley's general shrinkage of population. By 1883 it was down to 1,280 inhabitants (Martínez Gracida), and a hundred years later it had lost another third of its population; its total for 1982 was 864.

As early as 1966, Mary Elizabeth Smith, the friend who relayed Franco's lienzo discovery to me in 1974, proposed that the cattail glyph on the Coixtlahuaca lienzos represented San Miguel Tulancingo in the district of Coixtlahuaca. She based her belief on three of the lienzos— *Coixtlahuaca*, Lienzo A and *Tlapiltepec*—for she did not then have access to Seler II. Smith's suggestion is in the facsimile edition of *Codex Columbino* issued by the Sociedad Mexicana de Antropología, a publication in which she was a joint but independent author with Caso. Caso, however, was not ready to subscribe to her belief. He knew Tula, in Hidalgo, played a crucial role in early Mixtec history, and he did not want to close the door on the possibility that this cattail glyph might indicate that well-known and important northern city. Ever since Jiménez Moreno established that Tula, and not Teotihuacan, was the Tollan Xicocotitlan of legends and the early chronicals, Tula's position in history had become clearer and more detailed. At the time of Caso's death in 1970, he was still not convinced that this cattail glyph on the Coixtlahuaca lienzos represented such an insignificant place as San Miguel Tulancingo, Oaxaca. But the first volume of his *Reyes y Reinos de la Mixteca*, published 7 years after his death, reveals (1977, 132) that he had abandoned his idea that the glyph showed Tula, Hidalgo. "It seems, then," he wrote, "that the *Tule* to which these lienzos refer could not have been the Tula in the state of Hidalgo, only another place nearer to the region chocho-popoloca y mixteca." He could have had Cholula in mind.

Some history about Tula and after its fall is helpful. Jiménez Moreno provides it in his "Meso-America before the Totecs" in *Ancient Oaxaca* (1966, 3–82). Two salient facts are established by this masterly attempt at reconstructing a distant past, inadequately recorded and full of confusing claims. One is that many people migrated, with some migrations involving great distances. The other is that there was much intermingling in these migrations, some peaceful, some warlike, between people of high Mesoamerican culture and cruder people, ranging from barbaric nomads to primitive agriculturists. Three events contributed to especially massive migrations: the fall of Teotihuacan around 650; the revitalization of Cholula when it was conquered around 800 by the Olmeca-Xicallancas; and the fall of Tula around 1175.

The chronicles gives a bewildering variety of tribal names in connection with these migrations. Popolocas were said to be among the people at Teotihuacan. Teotihuacan refugees called Pipiles were said to have taken refuge in Cholula. The most warlike of the Olmeca-Xicallancas who conquered Cholula were said to be Mixtec. Some claim the Pipiles, driven out by these tyrants, migrated as far south as Santa Lucia Cotzumalhuapa, taking Teotihuacan traits to Guatemala. Then the Pipiles, having acquired the knowledge of metallurgy, returned north. Now called Nonoalcos, they stopped at Tulancingo—not San Miguel Tulancingo in Oaxaca, but another place of the same name in the state of Hidalgo. It was much older, as Florencia Müller and César Lizardi Ramos discovered, when they excavated there between 1955 and 1958 (Müller and Lizardi 1959). This Tulancingo dated back to the first records of agriculture around 1500 B.C., and went on through two Ticoman horizons and preclassic Teotihuacan up to Teotihuacan IV. Part of the Teotihuacan Empire, under the influence of Chupicuaro culture for six centuries, (beginning in 300 B.C.), it had derived importance as "the gateway to the Huasteca and the highly prized produce of the coastal regions" (Davies 1980, 228). When Michael and Elizabeth Snow excavated there in 1968 they found nothing they could describe as "Toltec" (Snow 1969, 33).

At the start of the tenth century, Nonoalcos at this northern Tulancingo moved to Tula and there, around 920, they mixed with the less cultured Toltec-Chichimecas in building a successor to Teotihuacan as a center dominating Mesoamerica. The fall of Tula more than two centuries later, was caused by internal dissension between adherents of the gods Tezcatlipoca and Quetzalcoatl. Refugees from Tula created a new center of Toltec culture at Culhuacan in the Valley of Mexico. Others invaded the Popoloca area between Puebla and the Mixteca Alta, and settled around Tehuacan and Teotitlan del Camino; a region said to have been populated earlier by refugees from Teotihuacan. Just south of the Popoloca area were people who spoke Chocho.

All this information contributes much uncertainty about the ethnic antecedents of the people of the Coixtlahuaca Valley. It also suggests there were many *tollans* those people might have come from—Teotihuacan, Cholula, Tulancingo, Tula. There is support of the case for Tulancingo in that the massive *Gazetteer* of Mexican names assembled in 1956 by the United States Board of Geographic Names, reports Tulancingo, Hidalgo, as the only town with the same name as Tulancingo, Oaxaca. The coincidence is remarkable because, in contrast, there are scores of places starting with variants of Tula or Tule.

The importance of Teotihuacan, Cholula, Tulancingo, Hidalgo, and Tula helps explain the popularity of *tollan* as a place name. In her *Picture Writing from Ancient Southern Mexico*, Dr. Smith, in discussing "Place Signs with the Marsh-Grass Motif" (70–75), makes another important point. *Tollan* did not mean only "place of the marsh grass." It also meant "a congregation of many artists and craftsmen," "a place of fertility and abundance," and a "great site and center of population." Accordingly, it was bestowed on, or adopted by, a number of important centers, besides Tula and the two Tulancingos. Cholula and Tenochtitlan, too, were both considered *tollans*, and Dr. Smith gives details from pictorial manuscripts showing how some glyphs for these centers include cattails. She also located places with cattails in their glyphs in Mixtec documents. Before discussing these Mixtec examples, however, more groundwork should be laid.

Another reason for the popularity of *tollan*, or variants of it, was that many people believed *tollan* was the name of their original homeland. When they migrated they liked to incorporate the name in their new homes. Nigel Davies's cautionary words in his *The Toltecs Until the Fall of Tula* are worth noting here (339):

It is of course perfectly possible that, just as in Highland Guatemala, so in the Mixteca the concept of Tollan, of Tulán, comes to play a significant part in the local mythology, as indicating more a legendary place of origin. Thus, even if Tollan Xicocotitlan was too remote to persist in people's minds as a living metropolis, it could still figure in the local version of the universal place-of-origin saga. . . . Thus it would seem not entirely illogical to question whether at least certain Mixtec tule signs might not somehow be related to a place which would have been regarded in Mixtec legends as a general place of origin of the Mixtec tribes, just as Apoala was conceived as that of their gods. This would in no way indicate that such people had really come from Tollan, any more than did the Quichés or Cakchiquels. For the Mixtecs, as for the latter, the name Tollan could have become more a place of fable, a kind of original Garden of Eden, for which local counterparts also existed.

WHY THE GLYPHS DIFFER

We are now better able to face the question of why the glyph of Tulancingo should be so different on two sets of documents—a place of swiftly running water on *Ihuitlan* and *Tulancingo*, and probably the Selden Roll, and a place of cattails on *Coixtlahuaca*, Lienzo A, *Tlapiltepec* and Seler II. It should be added that the difference extends to more than visual symbols. Dates, too, are involved. Because four of the lienzos point to the importance to Tulancingo of year 6 Reed, day 6 Dog, one would assume this date would be sure to be found on Tulancingo's own lienzos. It bears eight dates, but, strikingly, 6 Reed, 6 Dog, is not one of them. The date it stresses, in common with *Ihuitlan*, is the one we established by correlating the information in Figure 3 and 5: the year 12 Serpent, day 5 Flint. Obviously these days in the 6 Reed year and the 12 Serpent one are both dates of fundamental importance to the community. Why should *Tulancingo* lack the date so prominently associated with the cattail temple platform? And why should the founders' date that *Tulancingo* shares with *Ihuitlan* be nowhere in evidence at the four cattail glyphs?

Is there a possibility that the disparate glyphs, using different symbols and featuring different dates, don't represent the same place after all? It is the known geographical accuracy of these lienzos (Parmenter 1982, 35–36), especially *Tlapiltepec*, that eliminates this doubt. On the lienzos showing Tulancingo with the cattail glyph, the relative location of the town to the other towns depicted is the same as is San Miguel Tulancingo's spatial disposition to valley towns on modern maps. How the divergent dates are ordered in time (which is earlier and how many decades separate them), how they correlate with the Christian calendar, and why each set of glyphs has one date and not the other—these are secrets that will have to be disclosed by history, not geography.

One explanation of towns having differing glyphs is that one glyph is a pictorial representation of the natives' name for their town in their own language, and the other a representation of the name given the town by speakers of Nahuatl. *Codex Mendoza*, with its rich store of glossed examples of glyphs, provides what for our purposes is a particularly good example. It does not include Tulancingo, Oaxaca, among its Mixtec places on page 43, but its page 30 (recto) includes Tulancingo, Hidalgo. There one finds a coordination of our town's name in Nahuatl, Tollintzinco, with a glyph expressing that name in pictorial terms (Figure 26). It does so by using *Tzintli*, Nahuatl for a human rump, as an ideograph for *tzin* (small), which we have seen as a reverential or affectionate diminutive. So the pictured rump and a sedge plant (*tollin*) can be read, as

61

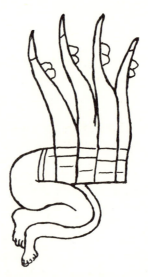

FIGURE 26. **The glyph of Tulancingo, Hidalgo, as shown on the** *Codex Mendoza.*

Cooper Clark asserts (1938) as "in the small sedges." Were it not for the gloss, however, we would not know the Mendoza glyph depicted a plant related to a cattail. The cylindrical inflorescence is not shown. The leaves indicate some kind of a plant, but not necessarily a sedge.

No rump appears in the glyphs of Oaxaca's Tulancingo. Perhaps this is an indication that the inhabitants of the town never called it by a Nahuatl name when they referred to it among themselves. But thanks to the study of María Teresa Fernández de Miranda (1961, 446) we do have some linguistic guidance. The Mixtec name of San Miguel Tulancingo, according to Smith (1973, 70), "is not recorded in any of the standard sources of Mixtec place names." Sra. Miranda, however, found a Chocho name for it—*ninga xingo*, which she translates as *al otro lado de la barranca* ("at the other side of the ravine"). Before returning to this, we should examine other factors that give clues to why the glyphs on the Coixtlahuaca documents differ.

In its disposition of elements and manner of drawing, *Tulancingo* is certainly the latest document under consideration. That *Ihuitlan* is later than the others is not apparent stylistically, but there is a strong historical sign that it is. The ruler list of one of the great dynasties of the valley, that of Lord 1 or 8 Wind, ends on four of the lienzos, *Tlapiltepec, Seler II, Coixtlahuaca* and Lienzo A—with the same ruler, the successor of the 10 Serpent, shown to the right in Figure 16 as the ruler of Stone with Eye-Coixtlahuaca. This last ruler, Lord 6 Water (Fig. 27), is the hero we have already met, though not by an English version of the Mixtec rebus for his name. Caso has identified him as Atonaltzin (1977, 134) the ill-fated consolidator of Coixtlahuaca whose downfall in the mid-1400s was brought about by the invading forces of Montezuma the Elder. His wife,

FIGURE 27. Atonaltzin, Lord 6 Water, the ruler of Coixtlahuaca, who was killed during the Aztecs' second and successful attack on his fief. His wife, Lady 7 Serpent, is thought to have been a prize of the conqueror, Montezuma the Elder. This representation of Atonaltzin is from the lienzo of Ihuitlan.

Lady 7 Serpent, hardly lives up to her reputation for great beauty in this portrait, but other things support Caso's identification. His name in Nahuatl, Atonaltzin, meaning "Water Day," squares with his pictorially represented name. More important, his final position on four lienzos shows that the succession of rulers leading up to him stopped with him. Thus four lienzos, without depicting their Aztec enemies, or showing Atonaltzin being killed, confirm the Aztec chroniclers that Atonaltzin's death ended an ancient line. Probably those who commissioned these four lienzos did not want to trace the history of Coixtlahuaca beyond its rule by their own forebears. But the Aztecs did not destroy Coixtlahuaca — that would be killing the goose that laid the golden egg. Nor did they impose Aztec rulers. Rather they let other regional lords, either Mixtec or Chocho, continue as rulers provided they paid heavily for the status. The lienzo of Ihuitlan (Frontispiece) shows four rulers succeeding 6 Water at Coixtlahuaca. So *Ihuitlan* if not painted later than the lienzos of the cattail glyph, certainly brings the valley historically closer to the arrival of the Spaniards than any of the dates given for the downfall of Atonaltzin. Whatever *Ihuitlan's* date of creation, then, like *Tulancingo*, it is closer in time to the arrival of the Spaniards than *Tlapiltepec* or Seler II. This cannot be inferred of *Coixtlahuaca* or Lienzo A, which both show the Spaniards arriving on their horses. The cattail glyphs on them, however, are relatively negligible. Small cattail glyphs, or none at all, may imply greater interest in dynastic history within the valley than in epochal events farther back in time, possibly related to origin elsewhere. Perhaps one can say that the lienzos of the cattail glyph stress Tulancingo's "ancient" history, while those of the running water glyph are concerned chiefly with its "modern" history.

This difference in time focus is also reflected in the character of the glyphs. For the people of Tulancingo in the sixteenth century the water glyph depicted the environment they knew, the good stream rushing through the valley in which they lived. Conversely, the cattail had nothing to do with their narrow place between the high mountains. Had there been a conference on changing their glyph (as modern manufacturers sometimes change their marketing symbols), one can almost imagine the arguments of those proposing change, and those opposing it.

The latter might have argued: we have had the tule as the chief element of our glyph ever since our ancestors settled here. They brought it with them and adopted it at the same time as they assumed our name, Dear Place of Tule. They chose the name and the symbol for the same reason. Some say our ancestors came from Tula in the north. Others claim it was from our namesake Tulancingo, older than Tula. Others argue for Cholula, which is much nearer. Others have lost all certainty. It was so long ago that we cannot be sure which *tollan* it was. Perhaps the cattail refers to a legendary place of origin, as we have heard it does with other towns, and does not refer to a historical town that can be placed geographically. Certainty on this point is not necessary for us to cherish the cattail symbol. Retaining it has the further advantage of preserving one of the most important events in our history—the time when our ruler-priest—for we were an important religious center, as well as an important town—was besought by other valley rulers so they could feel free, if he gave his sanction and blessing, to subdue Coixtlahuaca.

Fanciful or not, one can see a modern parallel in such a debate when Canadian nationalists campaigned in the 1950s to change their flag to eliminate the Union Jack of Great Britain as one of its elements. What was proposed was a flag featuring the leaf of a native tree—the maple. And the proponents of a red maple leaf on a white field won. Perhaps neither side won in Tulancingo, and some artists continued to designate the town with a cattail and some with a running stream.

Whatever the outcome, the differences in the glyphs do not prove we are dealing with different places. Our lienzos show that other towns, too, had widely differing glyphs—including Ihuitlan, Tulancingo's principal neighbor. Its glyph on its own lienzo and on *Tulancingo* (Figs. 13 and 14), each with a massive serpent, and an axe planted butt down in a hill, is recognizably the same, even though its elements are drawn differently, and each has an element not on the other—down-sloping feathers in one case, and a human head in the other. Looking at Figure 28, we see the glyph of Ihuitlan on the lienzo of Tlapiltepec, and this little church with a buttressed bell tower is associated with the rulers that Ihuitlan and Tulancingo shared in their early days (Fig. 9, left). The church replaces the pagan serpent, and the axe is gone. The feathers, too, are modified. Instead of running raggedly down the hill on either side of the serpent, (Fig. 13) they are layered decorously to form a feather carpet, which has

FIGURE 28. **The glyph of Ihuitlan Plumas as shown on the lienzo of Tlapiltepec. The black serpent is replaced by a Christian church.**

two down balls below, looking to the modern viewer almost like turnips. Although it preserves the feathers, indicating Ihuitlan's great feather market, this instance, then, also shows the adoption of a revised glyph closer to a present reality than an old belief.

As we know from the two glossed Ihuitlan's on *Ihuitlan* (Frontispiece)— Pinoyalco Ihuitlan of the pre-Columbian ball court and Santiago yuitla of the Christian church—the site of this town was changed. Besides theorizing that Tulancingo's alternate glyphs represented different things— the cattail glyph, a sacred place, and the palace-water one showing where its rulers lived—Dr. Smith also suggested[4] a shift of the town might have caused the dualism. One glyph might apply to an earlier site, the other to a more recent one. This is plausible. Town sites were often altered, especially after the Spaniards began re-locating settlements. Supplementing the Ihuitlan shift, Joyce Bailey (1972) demonstrated there was a site change of Tejupan, the Place of the Jewel (Fig. 25), located as a neighbor of Tulancingo on three of the valley lienzos. At Tejupan there is archaeological proof that Teiupam Viejo was higher up the slopes of its guarding hills than present-day Santa Caterina Tejupan.

The Chocho name for Tulancingo, "the other side of the river," surely implies a move. And Nieto Angel names three sites near the present San Miguel Tulancingo where the town might have been located previously. The first, Cerro de la Campana, was on the top of a hill six kilometers

---

[4] Letter to author, 2 January 1986.

away because of the bell believed to be buried there. This occupancy is supported by archaeological remains: streets, houses, domestic utensils, and what Nieto called a church and a town hall. He repeats the popular tradition that this location was abandoned because the patron saint would not accept it, and Christian priests backed the saint's decision. The second settlement, with the Chocho name *Cuñianashingu*, was on another hill top three and a half kilometers nearer the present town. Sherds of ancient clay utensils have been found here, too. Without mentioning the information in Martinez Gracida's *Cuadros Sinopticos* (61) that the viceregal government gave titles and rights to several communities drawn together to Tulancingo's present site in 1751, Nieto names a third earlier Tulancingo as being at El Calvario, where for ages the town has celebrated the religious festivities of Holy Week. Whatever the shifts, "the other side of the river" applies aptly to the present Tulancingo, and, because Agua Dulce flows so copiously through that ravine, the running water glyph is still graphically suitable.

More than forty years ago, Ignacio Bernal conducted archaeological excavations in Coixtlahuaca (Bernal 1948), exploring thirty-nine burials in a pre-Columbian residential area near the ceremonial center. He found evidence of the Aztec occupation, as well as considerable pottery decorated in the style of the Mixtec codices and seven stone houses with stucco floors. Obviously further study is needed in the valley, for Bernal also found pre-Columbian remains in Tlacotepec (adjoining Ihuitlan), Tlapiltepec and Suchixtlahuaca. When such work is undertaken, it is to be hoped the ruins of La Campana will be included. What the lienzos of the valley have shown about Tulancingo proves those ruins, no less than those of Ñaate and Veinte Idolos, warrant attention.

THE QUESTION OF 4 JAGUAR

When every detail of the lienzo of Tulancingo has been photographed clearly, and the townspeople who cooperated with Nieto in his monograph have assisted in its study as much as they can, including revealing ancient documents they hold,[5] the lienzo will yield more information than I have drawn from it. As a matter of courtesy, I have deliberately left untouched its glosses in Chocho, its glyphs other than those for Tulancingo and Ihuitlan, and its dates, other than the Year 12 Flint, day 5 Serpent, which is different from the Year 6 Reed, day 6 Dog, the founding date associated with the cattail glyph. And I have not given the names of all its personages, an area of study for some future scholar. Nor have I done any research in archives. Although I have learned nothing about *Tulancingo*'s use in disputes over boundaries, it might have been involved in land litigation at one time or another. The possibility exists because over the years many Mexican towns, hoping to support their land claims, have taken their pictorial document to court. The possibility that Tulancingo did, however, is slight because Carlos Rincón Mautner who studied a number of the town's land documents, did not find a reference to the lienzo being used as evidence in a court case.

Two more points elucidated by the lienzo deserve comment. One is Tulancingo's relationship—or lack of relationship—with pictorial manuscripts from beyond the area of Coixtlahuaca. Specifically, to check if *Tulancingo* sheds light on whether the 4 Jaguar who, in Codex Nuttall and other Mixtec deer hide codices, is shown as a co-conqueror with 8 Deer of Tilantongo (Jansen 1978, 15), is one or more of the 4 Jaguars on the Coixtlahuaca documents. The point is important because positive connections between the deer hide screenfolds that pay so much attention to 8 Deer and the lienzos of Coixtlahuaca have yet to be found.

The search for these connections originated with Zelia Nuttall's discovery of Lord 8 Deer, in Oxford in 1898 as she was studying the codex named in her honor when the Peabody Museum at Harvard, Mass., published a reproduction of it in 1902. Eight Deer was a major pre-Columbian warrior, who is shown in Figure 29 wearing the helmet of a jaguar knight, and who, as Mrs. Nuttall discovered, was repeatedly depicted with a personal name as well as a calendrical one—a hook emerging from a disk that she rightly interpreted as a claw of a feline. This personal name enabled her to discern that 8 Deer "Tiger Claw"

---

[5] Personal communication from Jesús Franco Carrasco, 27 October 1974. Nieto attests to documents dated 1521, 1750, 1775, and 1821.

FIGURE 29.   Lord 4 Jaguar starting on a war of conquest of many places in the Coixtlahuaca Valley. His personal name is above him. It is a flute in the form either of a jaguar
or a serpent. The drawing is from the lienzo of Tlapiltepec.

recurred often in her codex, having a number of adventures and conquering many places. By calling him to the scholarly world's attention
(Nuttall 1902), she was able to demonstrate that the document was a historical record, and that 8 Deer was not mythical, but historical. Codex
Nuttall was one of the small body of Mexican codices painted on deer
hide and preserved in Europe. Mrs. Nuttall's discoveries helped interpret
them all, including, most importantly, how to distinguish those that
were historical from the five that were religious. Having found many
clues as to how the historical ones could be deciphered, she made a
wrong geographical connection for her codex. Because she was convinced that 8 Deer's conquests were in Aztec territory, she contended his
activities were in the Valley of Mexico.

That 8 Deer was more important than it first seemed has been proved
by more recent scholars who have found him on more of the deer hide
codices than Mrs. Nuttall did and they also have coordinated his various
appearances. It was not until 1949, however, that Caso made the link
between geography and history that, with the facts it established about
the historical codices, has become the most important link in deciphering
the Mixtec pictorial manuscripts. Through study of the personages on
the post-Conquest map of Teozacoalco (Caso 1949), he proved 8 Deer
came from Tilantongo in the Mixteca Alta.

Fourteen years later, Mary Elizabeth Smith forged another important connection between history and geography (1963, 276–88). She located the place where 8 Deer had the septum of his nose pierced so that, young as he was at the time, he could wear an ornament signifying he was a great lord. It was Tulixtlahuaca, formerly dependent on San Pedro Jicayan—significantly, in the Mixteca Costa. Her evidence thereby established that 8 Deer was active in the Costa as well as in the Alta, making him a wider-ranging figure than had been supposed. Since similar nose-piercings are shown in *Colombino* and *Nuttall*, her identification of the location of one helped fill out 8 Deer's biography. The important figure who did the nose piercing at Tulixtlahuaca was Lord 4 Tiger, "Face of the Night," as she translated his personal name.

Dr. Smith's complex of discoveries was one of the great coups in modern Mixtec studies—a major event in the process of correlating geography and pre-Columbian history. Those studies have long been crippled because of the separation of geography from history. It is an irony that the preciousness of the Mixtec pictorial manuscripts—their artistic value, which caused the Conquistadors to send the finest to Europe as princely gifts; their value to pre-Columbian religious lore, which caused the destruction of so many by Spanish priests, and their legal value for those hoping to benefit from them in court cases—has been largely responsible for their separation from their rightful owners. Wealthy collectors have removed them so far from their origin that their provenance has been forgotten while looters and other unscrupulous persons have stolen them. Zealous guardians in the towns have taken them so completely out of circulation that they have been "lost" to all but insiders. Such behavior has deprived us of the sort of input geography can give ancient records.

What importance for the lienzo of Tulancingo has proof that 8 Deer's early nose piercing was at Tulixtlahuaca, a surviving town on the Pacific coast? The importance derives from Tulixtlahuaca—not surprisingly because of its name—having cattails on its glyph. Dr. Smith located three places with cattails on their glyphs on three screenfolds associated with 8 Deer. In her nomenclature, a 4 Tiger appears at each of these localities. Tulixtlahuaca on *Colombino* is the first she discusses. *Bodley* yielded a second and also showed this other glyph with the cattail several times, with its depiction of 4 Tiger's piercing of 8 Deer's nose there on page 9. Despite the presence of the same personages, she does not think the place of the similar ceremony is the coastal city of Tulixtlahuaca. Since that is probably the case, she prefers to give the problematic *Bodley* location a provisional descriptive name, "Cattail Frieze."

The third Mixtec place with a cattail in its glyph studied by Dr. Smith was on pages 4 and 14 of *Becker I*. Because each of these *Becker* representations showed part of a serpent with an upswept feathered tail, she identified this place as Tulancingo in the Valley of Coixtlahuaca. Dr. Smith thinks that 4 Tiger was associated with this place also, though in her book, *Picture Writing*, she did not say how.

Nancy P. Troike offered an explanation for the association in her Ph.D. thesis, "The Codex Colombino-Becker," lamentably still unpublished. She did so in concentrating on its page 4 showing the visit of 8 Deer and 4 Jaguar to a personage whom she then interpreted—following Caso's lead—as the Sun God, but who by the 1980s she no longer considered either god, or man related to the sun. On this page, 8 Deer and 4 Jaguar kneel facing each other on either side of a U-shaped depression partially dividing the elaborate bases on which they kneel. Each seems to point with a forefinger into the depression. In the lower tier of the page are three large place glyphs, the one on the right being that identified by Dr. Smith as Tulancingo of Coixtlahuaca. The representation of the same place on page 14 shows a man meeting 4 Jaguar there. Dr. Troike comments:

This marks the first appearance of this site in the extant Colombino-Becker since it was shown in the final scene of the journey to the Sun God (Becker 4.) Since it does not appear to be the same locality as that at which 8 Deer's representatives had met 4 Jaguar many years before (Colombino 9–12), it is not clear whether 4 Jaguar had now additionally acquired control over it, or if the meeting is only held there. (p. 476).

The 4 Jaguars depicted as the eleventh and seventeenth lords in the ruler list of Miltepec (4 Jaguar II is in Fig. 16) are not the only 4 Jaguars on the Coixtlahuaca documents. Lienzo A and *Coixtlahuaca* duplicate each other in showing close to their inner borders three conquests (of a Hill of the Dove, a Hill of the Eagle, and a Hill of the Shell) by a 4 Jaguar whose relationship is not securely established with three of the documents' other 4 Jaguars, but whose victories accentuate how much war there was in the valley. *Tlapiltepec* provides an especially conspicuous 4 Jaguar at the center of its left edge (Fig. 30). This conqueror, who may or may not be the victor over the dove, eagle and shell hills, is presented as a mighty warrior, with a shield and upraised obsidian sword, embarking on a string of conquests so long it runs vertically a considerable way up the lienzo.

Dr. Smith does not think this 4 Tiger, the historic figure that *Talpiltepec* shows starting a ten-year war, is the 4 Tiger shown with 8 Deer contemplating Tulancingo on *Colombino-Becker*. "If 4-Tiger is a historical personage," she asks, "how can he be the eleventh century ruler of Tulancingo of Coixtlahuaca, as Becker I indicates, and the eleventh century ruler of Tulixtlahuaca of Jicayán as is stated in Colombino?" (Smith 1973, 74).

She argues that, he can't, and points out how the only consistency that can be found among the 4 Tigers who pierce noses (*Bodley* also shows a 4 Tiger piercing the nose of a 4 Wind, the murderer of 8 Deer, at "Cattail Frieze") was through abandoning the hypothesis that he was a ruler in any traditional sense. Her alternate hypothesis is that perhaps various 4 Tigers were priests impersonating the deity 4 Tiger. That he is never shown with a wife is among her arguments that this apparently

FIGURE 30. Lord 8 Deer "Tiger Claw" as he appears on page 43 of Codex Nuttall.

multiple personality was not a historical ruler. Moreover, his parents are not shown, nor is he depicted as a father.

The evidence that made me change my mind about the 4 Jaguar association with 8 Deer with any of the 4 Jaguars on the Coixtlahuaca documents was that two of these obviously historical characters had wives. Both Seler II and *Tlapiltepec* show the first 4 Jaguar's wife was Lady 7 Wind, and the same two lienzos show 4 Jaguar II's wife was 2 Dog. Separated by six generations, both 4 Jaguars, had many descendants.

The personal name of the Coixtlahuaca documents' most conspicuous 4 Jaguar (Figure 30) is another weighty piece of evidence. Caso calls it "Flauto de Serpiente." To me, the ears of the head at the end of the musical instrument are more suggestive of a jaguar than a serpent, but there can be no doubt that a wind instrument is represented. No matter which animal head is indicated, nowhere is this personal name shown in conjunction with the many representations of 8 Deer's associate. Conversely, the personal name of 8 Deer's associate, "Face of the Night," is not given to any of the Coixtlahuaca 4 Jaguars.

Another factor contributing to my skepticism about 8 Deer's associate, 4 Jaguar, being the conqueror of so many towns in the Coixtlahuaca

Valley is finding no sign that 8 Deer, widely as he spread his domain, ever entered this Coixtlahuaca valley. Surely if the valley's 4 Jaguar was a co-conqueror with 8 Deer, the Coixtlahuaca documents would have preserved some evidence of its local hero being an ally of the even greater conqueror from Tilantongo. Proof of such an alliance would have redounded still further to 4 Jaguar's glory.

Dr. Troike ignores the deity impersonator hypothesis and has little difficulty accepting 4 Jaguar as a historical figure. And she has worked out an ingenious, plausible and consistent narrative of the relationship of the historical 4 Jaguar with both 8 Deer and 4 Wind, 8 Deer's murderer. But she too, is skeptical about the great nose-piercer being a Coixtlahuaca lord. In the first appearance of the cattail place with the feathered serpent tail on Colombino-Becker, 4 Jaguar, she says, merely looks toward the glyph. In the other appearance of the glyph in the codex he is said to meet a man (with all characteristics erased) *at* the glyph place, not that he controlled the place. And it wasn't here that he was shown earlier.

The correlation of Mixtec and Christian dates has grown more refined with time, but it is still tricky. Some dates that have become fairly well established, however, also throw doubt on the two 4 Jaguars being identical. If one of Coixtlahuaca's 4 Jaguars benefitted from the conquest of Coixtlahuaca, which Caso in the first volume of his *Reyes y reinos de la Mixteca* (Caso, 49) placed in 1265, he was a figure appearing two centuries later than the 4 Jaguar associated with 8 Deer, for 1065–1115 is now accepted by many as 8 Deer's life span.

Caso did not believe the 4 Jaguar associated with 8 Deer was on the Coixtlahuaca lienzos (1979, 321–323). Nor was he convinced that the 4 Jaguars I have drawn were the same person either. To him 4 Jaguar, "Flauto de serpiente," (Fig. 30) was an earlier conqueror, and he was not certain whether 4 Jaguar, the conquering ruler of Remolino Coixtlahuaca (Fig. 16) was 4 Jaguar I of Miltepec or 4 Jaguar II, with the latter being more likely.

This brings us to the lienzo of San Miguel Tulancingo's contribution to the problem of the 4 Jaguars. Granted, it does not show Tulancingo's rulers as completely as *Ihuitlan* does; nor does it show the priests supplicating the lost-named ruler on the year 6 Reed, day 6 Dog—neither does it show any of the 4 Jaguars. As a glance at Figure 9 will show, no 4 Jaguar is listed as a Tulancingo ruler on either *Tulancingo* or *Ihuitlan*. Nor does *Tulancingo* show a 4 Jaguar among the three couples outside the Tulancingo succession, who are probably rulers of neighboring towns. That there is no 4 Jaguar on the lienzo of Tulancingo reinforces that in depictions of Tulancingo as the place of the platform with the cattail glyph on *Tlapiltepec*, Seler II, Lienzo A and *Coixtlahuaca*, 4 Jaguar is not included among their personages either.

The absence of the nose-piercing 4 Jaguar from *Tulancingo* may cast some doubt on Dr. Smith's identification of the glyph of the cattail and the serpent with the feathered tail on *Becker I* as signifying Tulancingo of Coixtlahuaca—strong as the visual evidence is. That absence from

Tulancingo also shows John Pohl's wise caution in his well-ordered descriptions of how the nose-piercing 4 Jaguar appears in the Mixtec codices. He calls 4 Jaguar "the Foreign Benefactor" and argues that lords of the Mixteca Alta came to him to have their rights to rule legitimized by being given nose jewels. The place where he operated was his home base said Pohl, who voted against Tulixtlahuaca (Dr. Smith's candidate for the nose-piercing place shown in *Colombino*) as a 4 Jaguar base. Pohl favored a candidate of his own. Though he did not rule out Cholula entirely, he implied that all the cattail places were the Chocho-speaking town of his choice, "tentatively identified as Tulancingo, a *sujeto* of Coixtlahuaca" (Pohl 1984, 139). If this was correct, a personage so important to the community as 4 Jaguar would be on Tulancingo's lienzo. That he is not, makes this a link of history and geography that is not likely to hold.

If San Miguel Tulancingo is not on Becker I, the lack of relationship between the 8 Deer codices and the Coixtlahuaca lienzos is emphasized. This *tollan* on Becker I, up to now, has seemed one of the few links appearing secure.

Two other important points elucidated by *Tulancingo* are much more obvious. The first is that by the time of its painting, the Spanish pacification of the valley was so complete that this lienzo dominated by the Christian church in its center, with six other churches, shows no sign of the warfare so prevalent in other valley documents. The other is that the present small progressive town of hard-working people, who have made good use of their limited arable soil, has an importance for the history of the Valley of Coixtlahuaca that has not been adequately recognized. In his 1961 study of *Ihuitlan*, Caso said nothing about Tulancingo, nor of the strangeness of his finding no reference to it on *Ihuitlan*. Because it is on *Ihuitlan*, however, a lot of information about Tulancingo is available that can be used to fill out and elucidate information about the town known to be on the other lienzos in cryptic form. Old and new information, when coordinated, has expanded the picture that illuminates all the lienzos, including that of Tulancingo itself. Our new picture also illuminates the total Mexican mosaic into which it fits. Furthermore, Tulancingo's commanding position on *Ihuitlan* reinforces the evidence of *Tlapiltepec* and Seler II that Tulancingo, Oaxaca, hitherto almost unknown, was once a key component—for religious reasons, as well as secular ones—in a cultural area that, with its wealth and historical importance, was far more notable than has yet been realized by students of the pre-Columbian past.

SUMMARY

In presenting an early description of the lienzo of San Miguel Tulancingo in Oaxaca this monograph has introduced to Mexican scholarship a document of considerable value. In itself, it has interest as a representative of a type of pictorial document that is proving especially useful as a scholarly resource for obtaining historical information difficult to access. As a painting, it illustrates a phase in a transitional art style that developed in the New World in the sixteenth century; it reflects, too, an earlier stage in Mexican picture writing. Its information is a contribution to what we know of a region that was important in pre-Columbian Mesoamerica. As a work of art, it is not as splendid as some of the other lienzos; nor does it have nearly as much information as such great ones as *Tlapiltepec*, Seler II and *Ihuitlan*. What it supplies on its own are a few dates, the glyphs of places in a corner of the region, and the names of seven generations of those who ruled Tulancingo before the coming of the Spaniards. But it provides more than its own contents. It holds mind-opening clues that, when combined with others, enable us to read far more than was heretofore possible into the eight lienzos that became known earlier.

Besides the knowledge that the family of documents to which it belongs is larger than was thought, and the district of Coixtlahuaca was more important, some of the specific things we now know are:

1. how Tulancingo is shown on seven of the lienzos;
2. how its glyph on three differs from its glyph on four;
3. which place "Agua" represents;
4. which glyph on *Ihuitlan* correctly represents Ihuitlan;
5. that the fourth major town on *Ihuitlan* (Q) is still to be identified;
6. how seven of the lienzos come from west of the valley, and only two from the east;
7. how the west and east lienzos differ in the history they record and ignore;
8. how much warfare there was between towns;
9. how the western towns kept together in an alliance;
10. how the original settlements of Ihuitlan and Tulancingo divided;
11. how the sequence of rulers on *Ihuitlan* determines their more fragmentary order on *Tulancingo* and *Tlapiltepec*;
12. how Tulancingo outdid Ihuitlan and Coixtlahuaca in providing spouses to ruling lineages of other places;
13. how the new religion of Quetzalcoatl entered the Coixtlahuaca Valley;
14. the four main places where it had administrative centers;

15. how the fourth was established ten generations later at Q;
16. pictorial evidence of the Aztec overthrow of Atonaltzin, who temporarily united Coixtlahuaca;
17. glimpses of the lives of a variety of 4 Jaguars;
18. how these 4 Jaguars seem to set the Coixtlahuaca lienzos apart from the better known 8 Deer Tilantongo codices on deer hide.

It is a respectable amount of material, much of which would not have been possible had there not been painted facts to correlate with geographical realities. The fit of the Tulancingo pieces depends largely on how they interlock with pieces on earlier known lienzos. Before the origin of *Tlapiltepec* was established, this sheet could yield only a portion of its information to interpret the other lienzos. Before the discovery of the two *Tequixtepecs* showing that the east of the valley also had many rulers, the idea of a western alliance could hardly have been conceived. And before the running water glyph of Tulancingo was confirmed, few of the jigsaw pieces could be fitted together with the provisional coherence they seem to have now.

Besides the information the study has ascertained, there are important questions it raises: who were the earlier inhabitants of the valley and can it be proved that some migrated from Tulancingo, Hidalgo?

Two major geographical mysteries remain: on *Ihuitlan*, the identity of the Place of the Digging Stick and the Loin Cloth, the Quetalcoatl administrative center I have called Q; on *Tlapiltepec* the River of the Palm Tree. Because of its role in the conquest of Coixtlahuaca, we need to know where the river was, and what it was called by its people. Nick Johnson shrewdly calculates that this information is necessary if confusion is to be eliminated from the tangled story of Coixtlahuaca's division into four fiefs.

Tulancingo's conflicting founding dates present historical mysteries. Which was earlier, the year 6 Reed, day 6 Dog of the cattail glyph, or the year 12 Flint, day 5 Serpent of the running water glyph? There are many indications that the 6 Reed date is the more ancient, and I believe it is. But were they close in time, or centuries apart? And where do they correlate with the Christian calendar? These valley lienzos have many insights yet to be discovered with further study.

BIBLIOGRAPHY

BAILEY, JOYCE W.
1972   Map of Texupa (Oaxaca) 1579: A Study of Form and Meaning. *The Art Bulletin*, 54, No. 4: 452–472.

BARLOW, R. H.
1949   The Extent of the Empire of the Culhua Mexica, *Ibero-Americana: 28*, University of California Press, Berkeley and Los Angeles.

BERNAL, IGNACIO
1948   Exploraciones en Coixtlahuaca, Oaxaca, *Revista Mexicana de Estudios Antropológicos*, V: 10, 5–76, Mexico.

BRADOMÍN, JOSÉ MARÍA
1955   *Toponimia de Oaxaca: crítica etimológica*. Mexico.

BURLAND, COTTIE A.
1955   The Selden Roll: An Ancient Mexican Picture Manuscript in the Bodleian Library at Oxford. *Monumenta Americana 2* (Cottie A. Burland, comment. Gerdt Kutscher, bibliography). Verlag. Gebr. Mann., Berlin.

CASO, ALFONSO
1949   El mapa de Teozacoalco, *Cuadernos Americanos*, VII: 5, 3–40.
1954   *Interpretación del Códice Gómez de Orozco*. Talleres de Impresión de Estampillas y Valores, Mexico.
1960a   The Historical Value of the Mixtec Codices, *Boletín de estudios oaxaqueños* 16. Museo Frissell, Mitla, Oaxaca.
1960b   *Interpretación del Códice Bodley 2858*. Sociedad Mexicana de Antropología, Mexico.
1961   Los lienzos mixtecos de Ihuitlan y Antonio de León, *Homenaje a Pablo Martínez del Rio en el XXV aniversario de la edición de "Los origenes americanos"*: 237–274. Instituto Nacional de Antropología e Historia, Mexico.
1966   *Interpretación del Códice Colombino/Interpretation of the Codex Colombino*. Sociedad Mexicana de Antropología, Mexico.
1977   *Reyes y reinos de la Mixteca I*. Fondo de Cultura Económica, Mexico.
1979   *Reyes y reinos de la Mixteca 2*. Fondo de Cultura Económica, Mexico.

CLARK, JAMES COOPER, ed. and trans.
1938   *Codex Mendoza: The Mexican Manuscript Known as the Collection of Mendoza and Preserved in the Bodleian Library, Oxford*, 3 vols. London.

DAHLGREN, BARBRO
1966   *La Mixteca: Su Cultura e Historia Prehispánicas*. Universidad Autonoma de Mexico, Mexico.

DAVIES, NIGEL
1977   *The Toltecs: Until the Fall of Tula*. University of Oklahoma Press, Norman.
1980   *The Toltec Heritage from the Fall of Tula to the Rise of Tenonchtilan*. University of Oklahoma Press, Norman.

FERNÁNDEZ DE MIRANDA, MARÍA TERESA
1961   Toponimia Popoloca, *A William Cameron en el vigesimoquinto aniversario del Instituto Lingüístico de Verano*, pp. 411–447, Mexico.

FLANNERY, KENT V., and JOYCE MARCUS, eds.
    1983 *The Cloud People: Divergent Evolution of the Zapotec and Mixtec Civilizations.* Academic Press, New York.
GATES, WILLIAM
    1931a Codex Ixtlan. *Maya Society Publication 3.* Johns Hopkins University Press, Baltimore.
    1931b Codex Meixueiro. *Maya Society Publication 4.* Johns Hopkins University Press, Baltimore.
GERHARD, PETER
    1972 *A Guide to the Historical Geography of New Spain.* Cambridge, England.
GLASS, JOHN B.
    1964 *Catalogo de la Colección de Codices,* Mexico.
GLASS, JOHN B., in collaboration with DONALD ROBERTSON
    1975 A Census of Native Middle American Pictorial Manuscripts, *Handbook of Middle American Indians 14* (Robert Wauchope and Howard F. Cline, eds.) 81–252. University of Texas Press, Austin.
JANSEN, MAARTEN, E.R.G.N. and MARGARITA GAXIOLA
    1978 Primera Mesa Redonda de Estudios Mixtecos: Síntesis de las Ponencias. *Estudios de Antropología e Historia.* Centro Regional de Oaxaca, Oaxaca.
JÍMENEZ MORENO, WIGBERTO
    1941 Tula y los Toltecas según las fuentes históricas, *Revista Mexicana de Estudios Antropólogios,* V: 2–3, 79–83.
    1966 Mesoamerica Before the Toltecs, *Ancient Oaxaca,* John Paddock, ed. Stanford University Press, Stanford, pp. 3–82.
JOHNSON, IRMGARD WEITLANER
    1967 Textiles (part IV), *The Prehistory of the Tehuacan Valley.* Douglas S. Byers, general editor. University of Texas Press, Austin, published for the Robert S. Peabody Foundation, Phillips Academy, Andover.
    1976 *Design Motifs on Mexican Indian Textiles.* (2 vols.) Academische Druck und Verlagsantalt Graz, Austria.
JOHNSON, NICHOLAS CARTER
    1992 The Genealogical Map on the Lienzo of Tlapiltepec: The Coixtlahuaca Region (M.A. thesis for the University of New Mexico, Albuquerque).
KÓNIG, VIOLA
    n.d. Der Lienzo Seler II (Coixtlahuaca II) und seine Stellung innerhalb der Coixtlahuaca Gruppe. Paper presented at the XLII International Congress of Americanists, Paris, 1976.
LEÓN, NICOLÁS, ed.
    1933 *Códice Sierra,* edited and translated with explanatory text by Nicolás León; introduction by Federico Gómez de Orozco, Museo Nacional, Mexico.
McANDREW, JOHN
    1965 *The Open-Air Churches of Sixteenth-Century Mexico.* Harvard University Press, Cambridge, Mass.
MARTÍNEZ GRACIDA, MANUEL, ed.
    1883 Colección de Cuadros Sinopticos de los pueblos, haciendas y ranchos del estado libre y soberano de Oaxaca. *Anexo No. 50 a la Memoria Administrativa presentada al H. Congreso del Mismo et 17 de septiembre 1883.* Imp. del Estado, Oaxaca.
    1910/1987 *Los Indios Oaxaqueños y Sus Monumentos Aequeológicos,* Oaxaca, Oax.

MÜLLER, FLORENCIA and LIZARDI RAMOS, CÉSAR
1959 La Piramide 6 de Huapalcalco, Hidalgo, Mexico. *Actas del XXXIII Congreso Internacional de Americanistas, San José, 20–27 Julio 1958.* Costa Rica.
NIETO ANGEL, RAUL
1984 *Tulancingo, Hidalgo: Una comunidad rural de la mixteca alta.* Universidad Autónomo Chapingo, Mexico.
NUTTALL, ZELIA
1902 *Codex Nuttall: Facsimile of the Ancient Mexican Codex Belonging to Lord Zouche of Harynworth England.* (Zelia Nuttall, intro.) Harvard University, Peabody Museum, Cambridge.
PADDEN, R. C.
1967 *The Hummingbird and the Hawk.* Ohio State University Press, Columbia, O.
PADDOCK, JOHN, ed.
1966 *Ancient Oaxaca: Discoveries in Mexican Archaeology and History.* Stanford University Press, Stanford.
PARMENTER, ROSS
1961 20th Century Adventures of a 16th Century Sheet. The Literature on the Mixtec Lienzo in the Royal Onterio Museum. *Boletín de Estudios Oaxaqueños* 20. November 15. Museo Frissell, Mitla, Oaxaca.
1970 The Identification of Lienzo A: A Tracing in the Latin American Library of Tulane University. *Philological and Documentary Studies* 2 (3) Volume completed in 1977. Tulane University, Middle American Research Institute, New Orleans.
1982 Four Lienzos of the Coixtlahuaca Valley. *Studies in Pre-Columbian Art & Archaeology 26.* Dumbarton Oaks, Trustees for Harvard University, Washington, D.C.
n.d. "A Ninth Lienzo of the Coixtlahuaca Valley," Talk with slides at the Chicago meeting of the American Society for Ethnohistory in November 1989 (Unpublished Ms.).
n.d. "Tulancingo Identified on the Lienzo of Ihuitlan: a Bonanza from a Ninth Lienzo from the Coixtlahuaca Valley." Talk with slides at the Tulane University meeting of the 47th International Congress of Americanists on July 9, 1991, in New Orleans, La. (in press).
PETERSON, FREDERICK A.
1959 *Ancient Mexico.* Allen & Unwin, London.
POHL, JOHN M. P.
1984 "The Earth Lords: Politics and Symbolism of the Mixtec Codices" (Doctoral thesis for the University of California, Los Angeles).
RICKARDS, CONSTANTINE GEORGE
1915 Notes on the "Codex Rickards," *Journal de la Société des Americanistes* (n.s.), 10: 47–57
RINCÓN MAUTNER, CARLOS
n.d. "The Territory and Environment of San Miguel Tulancingo, Oaxaca, Mexico." Paper at the Association of American Geographers in April 1990 in Toronto, Ont., Canada.
ROBERTSON, DONALD
1959 *Mexican Manuscript Painting of the Early Colonial Period: The Metropolitan Schools.* Yale University Press, New Haven.
ROSS, KURT
n.d. *Codex Mendoza, Aztec Manuscript.* Miller Graphics. (Publication place not given.)

SMITH, MARY ELIZABETH
 1963   The Codex Colombino, a Document of the South Coast of Oaxaca, *Tlalocan*, IV: 3, 276–88.
 1966   Las glosas del Códice Colombino/The Glosses of Codex Colombino. Bound with Caso's *Interpretación del Códice Colombino.* Sociedad Mexicana de Antropología, Mexico.
 1973   *Picture Writing from Ancient Southern Mexico: Mixtec Place Signs and Maps.* University of Oklahoma Press, Norman.

SMITH, MARY ELIZABETH and PARMENTER, ROSS
 1991   *The Codex Tulane.* Middle American Research Institute, Tulane University, New Orleans, Louisiana.

SNOW, MICHAEL E. and SNOW, ELIZABETH F.
 n.d.   Report of the First Season of Archaeological Investigations in the Tulancingo Valley, Hgo., Mexico. Unpublished paper submitted to the Instituto Nacional de Antropología e Historia, Mexico, February, 1969.

SPORES, RONALD
 1967   *The Mixtec Kings and Their People.* University of Oklahoma Press, Norman.

TAYLOR, WILLIAM B.
 1974   Landed Society in New Spain: A View from the South. *Hispanic American Historical Review* 54: 387–413. Duke University Press, Durham, N.C.

TROIKE, NANCY P.
 1974   "The Codex Colombino-Becker" (Doctoral Dissertation, University of London).

UNITED STATES BOARD OF GEOGRAPHIC NAMES
 1956   *Gazetteer No. 15, Mexico, Official Standard Names.* Office of Geography, Department of the Interior, Washington, D.C.

INDEX